ASIAN INGREDIENT SUBSTITUTIONS:

FISH AND FRUIT, VEGGIES AND VITTLES, NOODLES AND NOSHES, SEASONINGS AND SAUCES, AND MORE

Jean B. MacLeod

MacLeod How-To Books

Asian Ingredient Substitutions:
Fish and Fruit, Veggies and Vittles, Noodles and Noshes, Seasonings and Sauces, and more

ISBN-13: 9780997446487

Library of Congress Control Number: 2018910392

To my family

A

ABALONE, FARMED, FRESH – 1 pound
- 8 ounces dried abalone/*pao yu*, soaked in water for 3 to 4 hours
- 1 pound French conch, tenderized like fresh abalone
- 1 pound fresh clam meat

ABURAGE See TOFU, DEEP-FRIED

AGAR/AGAR AGAR (gelling agent derived from seaweed) – 2 teaspoons powdered
- 3 tablespoons agar flakes or threads (increase soaking time to 10 to 15 minutes)
- 1 kanten freeze-dried agar bar torn into pieces (increase soaking time to 30 or more minutes)
- 1 tablespoon unflavored gelatin powder/1/4-ounce envelope (follow package directions)
- 4 sheets silver leaf gelatin (follow package directions)
- 2 1/2 teaspoons apple pectin powder (follow package directions)

AMARANTH GREENS/CHINESE RED SPINACH/YIN TSAI – 1 pound
- 1 pound Swiss chard leaves
- 1 pound small flat-leaf spinach or baby spinach
- 1 pound lamb's quarters/*bathua*
- 1 pound New Zealand spinach/warrigal greens
- 1 pound young pumpkin greens
- 1 pound quinoa greens
- 1 pound orach/mountain spinach

AMCHUR/AMCHOOR/GROUND MANGO POWDER (Indian souring agent) – 1 teaspoon See also MANGO, GREEN
- 1 section of sun-dried amchoor slice (remove before serving if added to curry)

- 1/2 teaspoon tamarind powder
- 1/3 teaspoon powdered citric acid (found in the canning section of the supermarket)
- 1 teaspoon ground sumac or powdered lemon peel
- 1 to 2 teaspoons very finely grated lemon zest (spread it out to dry slightly before using; for sprinkling as a garnish)

ANCHOVY SAUCE/MAM NEM (Vietnamese cooking condiment) – 1 tablespoon
- 2 teaspoons anchovy paste plus 1 teaspoon water

ARALIA/TARA NO ME/DUREUP (Japanese and Korean angelica tree buds) – 1 pound
- 1 pound young asparagus

ARAME, DRIED (Japanese mild shredded seaweed) – 1 ounce
- 1 ounce wakame (soak for 15 to 20 minutes; cut out the center rib, then slice the rest into thin ribbons)
- 1 ounce kiri kombu/long narrow kombu strands (soak for 10 minutes)
- 1 ounce alaria (saltier; soak for 30 minutes)
- 1 ounce hijiki (stronger tasting; soak for 10 minutes)

ARROWHEAD ROOT/DUCK POTATO/KATNISS/CHI GU, FRESH (starchy Asian vegetable) – I pound
- 1 pound small red or yellow boiling potatoes

ASAFETIDA/ASAFOETIDA/HING/PERUNKAYA (pungent Indian seasoning) – 1 teaspoon ground
- 1 teaspoon yellow asafetida powder (milder; contains turmeric)
- 1/2 teaspoon each onion and garlic powder

ASAM GELUGOR/ASAM KEPING (Malaysian acid fruit) *See KOKUM*

ASIAN BASIL *See BASIL, HOLY; BASIL, THAI*

ASIAN DIPPING SAUCE – 1/4 cup
Make Your Own Stir together 2 tablespoons each soy sauce and unseasoned rice vinegar, 1 teaspoon finely minced green onion, and a little grated fresh ginger.

ASIAN FISH PASTE, FERMENTED/PRESERVED FISH/PADEK/PRAHOK/ MAM CA SAC (Southeast Asian salty solid flavoring agent) – 1 teaspoon
- ☞ 1 teaspoon fermented shrimp paste: Filipino *bagoong,* Thai *kapi,* Indonesian *trassi/terasi* (more pungent), or Burmese *ngapi*
- ☞ 1 1/2 teaspoons French or Italian anchovy paste
- ☞ 1 whole salt-packed anchovy, deboned and mashed
- ☞ 2 oil-packed anchovies, rinsed and mashed
- ☞ 2 teaspoons Asian fish sauce
- ☞ 1 tablespoon Japanese red *inaka* miso or brown *hatcho* miso

ASIAN FISH SAUCE See FISH SAUCE; FISH SAUCE, VEGETARIAN; JAPANESE FISH SAUCE; THAI FISH SAUCE; VIETNAMESE FISH SAUCE

ASIAN LETTUCE See CHINESE LEAF LETTUCE

ASIAN PEAR/KOREAN PEAR/JAPANESE PEAR/NASHI/NAJU PAE – 1 medium
- ☞ 2 crisp pears, such as Bosc

ATTA/PATENT DURA FLOUR/CHAPATI FLOUR (Indian extra-fine soft whole-wheat flour) – 1 cup See also BESAN; MAIDA; ROTI, and URAD DAL FLOUR
- ☞ 1 cup whole-wheat pastry flour, sifted
- ☞ 1/2 cup each white whole-wheat flour and maida (Indian soft white flour), sifted
- ☞ 2/3 cup all-purpose flour and 1/3 cup finely ground whole-wheat flour, sifted before measuring to remove any coarse flakes

B

BAGOONG (Filipino seasoning) *See SHRIMP PASTE, FERMENTED*

BAMBOO LEAVES *See WRAPPERS FOR FOOD, NON-EDIBLE*

BAMBOO SHOOTS, DRIED/MANG KO *– 3 to 4 ounces (3-to-4-inch-wide strips)*
- 9 to 12 ounces fresh or canned bamboo shoots (less meaty; reduce the cooking time)

BAMBOO SHOOTS, FRESH/CHUKSUN/PHAI TONG/TAKENOKO *– 1 pound (1 large or 3 to 4 small)*
- 8 ounces canned whole bamboo shoots, drained and rinsed (To remove the tinny taste, blanch the bamboo shoots in boiling water for 1 minute and then rinse with cold water.)
- 8 ounces refrigerated vacuum-packed trimmed bamboo shoots
- 2 cups fresh peeled water chestnuts (about 10) or 1 (8-ounce) can water chestnuts, drained and rinsed
- 8 ounces jicama, peeled and cut into pieces
- 8 ounces tender fresh broccoli stems, cut into pieces

BANANA BLOSSOM/BUD/JANTUNG PISANG/HUAPLI/BAP CHUÓI/ MOCHA (Southeast Asian vegetable) *– 1 pound (1 medium)*
- 1 (19-ounce) can banana blossom in brine, drained and rinsed
- 1 large artichoke, trimmed, halved lengthwise, and choke removed (for cooking; lacks color)
- 1 pound red Belgium endives (about 2 to 3), halved lengthwise (for salads and garnish)
- 1 pound crisp red cabbage leaves, finely shredded (for salads and garnish; for color, not taste)

BANANA FLOUR/PISANG STARCH (Filipino plantain flour) – 1 tablespoon for thickening
- 2 teaspoons arrowroot powder
- 1 tablespoon superfine sweet rice flour/glutinous rice flour (such as Mochiko)

BANANA LEAF, FROZEN (food wrapper) See also WRAPPERS FOR FOOD, NON-EDIBLE
- Fresh or dried corn husks (smaller)
- Foil lined with large lettuce leaves, or other tender leaves
- Parchment paper

BANANA SAUCE/TAMIS ANCHANG (Filipino condiment) – 1 tablespoon
- 1 tablespoon ketchup

BASIL, HOLY/BAI KAPHRAO/BAI KRAPAU/BAI GRAPAO/TULSI – 1 tablespoon chopped fresh leaves
- 1 1/2 teaspoons chopped fresh mint and small-leafed Mediterranean basil (if using in a cooked dish, add at the last minute)
- 1 tablespoon chopped fresh Peruvian basil, Thai basil, or anise/licorice basil
- 1 teaspoon jarred holy basil paste or holy basil seasoning

BASIL, THAI/ASIAN BASIL/BAI HORAPHA – 1 tablespoon chopped fresh leaves
- 1 tablespoon chopped fresh holy basil or anise basil/licorice basil
- 1 1/2 teaspoons chopped small fresh regular/sweet basil leaves and small fresh mint leaves

BAY LEAF, INDIAN See CASSIA LEAF/CINNAMON LEAF/TEJ PATTA

BEAN SAUCE See BLACK BEAN SAUCE; CHILI BEAN SAUCE; CHINESE YELLOW/BROWN BEAN SAUCE; VIETNAMESE YELLOW BEAN SAUCE

BEAN THREAD NOODLES *See NOODLES, CELLOPHANE*

BEANS, FERMENTED, SALTED BLACK *See FERMENTED BLACK BEANS*

BEECH MUSHROOM/BROWN BEECH/PIOPPINI/SHIMEJI – 7 ounces
- 7 ounces golden enoki, oyster, or small cremini mushrooms

BEEF, SUKIYAKI OR SHABU-SHABU-STYLE (Japanese thinly sliced meat) – 1 pound
- 1 pound rib-eye, strip loin, or sirloin sliced paper-thin against the grain (partly freeze the meat first to make it easier to slice)
- 1 pound Korean bulgogi beef

BELACAN *See SHRIMP PASTE*

BELIMBING/SOUR FINGER CARAMBOLA/BELIMBING WULUH/ MAFUANG/KHE (Southeast Asian fresh or dried sour green fruit) – 4 ounces
- 4 ounces fresh or dried kabosu, sudachi, yuzu, or rhubarb stems

BENGALI FIVE-SPICE MIX/PANCH PHORON (Bengali seasoning) – 1/3 cup
Make Your Own Combine 1 tablespoon each black cumin seeds, fenugreek seeds, black or brown mustard seeds, nigella seeds, and fennel seeds; store in an airtight container in a cool, dry place.

BENITADE SPROUTS (Japanese maroon-colored garnish) – 1 cup
- 1 cup alfalfa sprouts (for the taste)
- 1 cup finely shredded red cabbage (for the color)

BERBERE (Ethiopian spice blend) – 1 tablespoon
- 1 tablespoon harissa powder or peri-peri seasoning (for powder blend)
- 1 tablespoon harissa (for paste blend)
- 2 teaspoons hot or bittersweet/semi-hot paprika plus 1 teaspoon Chinese chili garlic sauce (for paste blend)

BESAN/GRAM FLOUR/CHANNA FLOUR/FARINE DE POIS CHICHES (Indian chickpea flour) – 1 cup

- 1 cup coarse chickpea flour/*jada besan*, ground to a powder
- 1 cup stone-ground garbanzo bean flour or garbanzo–fava bean flour blend
- 1 cup Italian chickpea flour/*farine de ceci*, such as Bartolini or Lucini Italia (finer texture)
- 2/3 cup fine-grind cornmeal plus 1/3 cup all-purpose flour (for coating fried chicken or seafood)

Make Your Own Toast 3/4 cup dried chickpeas/Bengal gram in a dry skillet over medium heat for 3 minutes, stirring constantly. Cool, grind to a powder in a spice/coffee grinder, then sieve to remove the husks.

BETEL LEAF See WILD PEPPER LEAVES

BHUT JOLOKIA/NAGA VIPER/GHOST CHILI/COBRA CHILI (Northeast Indian hot chili pepper) – 1

- 1 Carolina Reaper, Trinidad Moruga Scorpion, or Scorpion Butch T chili (hotter)
- 1 Red Savina chili (hotter cultivar of the habañero)
- 1 habañero, Scotch bonnet, or goat chili (fruitier tasting)
- 1 teaspoon Ghost chili pepper powder or Carolina Reaper chili powder

BIRD'S EYE CHILI/THAI CHILI/PIRI PIRI, FRESH OR DRIED (Southeast Asian medium hot red chili) – 2 or 3

- 2 or 3 fresh (if available) or dried de árbol, pequín, or tepín
- 1 red, fresh serrano, cayenne, or jalapeño chili
- 1/2 fresh Scotch bonnet or habañero chili (hotter)
- 1 teaspoon Thai red pepper flakes or chile de árbol pepper flakes
- 1 to 2 teaspoons sambal oelek or other hot chili paste; reduce the salt in the recipe accordingly

BITTER MELON/BALSAM PEAR/FOO GWA/KARELA See SQUASH, ASIAN

BLACHAN/BLACAN/BALACHAN *See SHRIMP PASTE, FERMENTED*

BLACK BEAN GARLIC SAUCE (Chinese salty cooking condiment) – 1/3 cup
- 2 tablespoons each rinsed salted black beans, light soy sauce, and rice wine plus 1 minced garlic clove, mashed to a coarse paste

BLACK BEAN SAUCE/PASTE/DOUCHI JIANG (Chinese salty cooking condiment) – 1 tablespoon
- 1 tablespoon Chinese fermented black beans, rinsed, mashed, and then combined with 1 teaspoon soy sauce
- 1 tablespoon Japanese dark miso, such as *hatcho*, or Korean soybean paste/*doenjang*

BLACK BEANS, FERMENTED *See FERMENTED BLACK BEANS*

BLACK SALT *See SALT, BLACK*

BOK CHOY/WHITE MUSTARD CABBAGE/CHINESE WHITE CABBAGE/ PAK CHOY – 1 pound
- 1 pound choy sum, Swiss chard, Savoy cabbage, napa cabbage, or leggy stalks of romaine lettuce
- 1 pound baby bok choy (sweeter; less fibrous)

BOMBAY DUCK/BOMBIL (Indian sun-dried salted fish) – 1 pound
- 1 pound salt cod

BONITO FLAKES/SKIPJACK TUNA, DRIED *See FISH FLAKES, DRIED*

BOUILLON – 1 cup
- 1 beef bouillon cube, 1 teaspoon beef bouillon granules, or 1 envelope instant broth, dissolved in 1 cup boiling water
- 1 seasoning packet from a 3-ounce-package beef-flavored ramen noodles dissolved in 1 cup boiling water
- 4 teaspoons dark miso (or 5 teaspoons light) added to 1 cup very

hot (not boiling) water a little at a time and stirred until smooth
- 1 porcini-flavored bouillon cube or 1 teaspoon wild mushroom bouillon granules dissolved in 1 cup boiling water
- 1 cup water plus a little soy sauce for flavor

BOUILLON CUBE, BEEF – 1.
- 4 teaspoons Japanese dark miso, such as *hatcho*; Korean soybean paste/*doenjang*; or tamari

BROTH, BEEF – 1 cup
- 1/2 cup each consommé and water
- 1 cup boiling water plus one of the following: 1 reduced-sodium bouillon cube, 1 envelope instant broth or granules, or 3/4 teaspoon beef soup base or gluten-free beef-flavored base (use half the amount for light meat or light broth)
- 2 teaspoons tamari or soy sauce added to 1 cup water
- 1 tablespoon noodle soup base, such as Kikkoman brand, added to 1 cup water
- 1 seasoning packet from a 3-ounce-package beef-flavored ramen noodles dissolved in 1 cup boiling water
- 2 teaspoons Maggi Seasoning added to 1 cup water
- 3/4 teaspoon beef extract or concentrated beef broth, such as Bovril, Better than Bouillon Beef Base, or Home Again, dissolved in 1 cup boiling water

BROTH, CHICKEN – 1 cup
- 1 cup canned or boxed reduced-sodium chicken broth, no-salt chicken stock, "no-chicken" broth/chicken-flavored vegetarian broth, plus 1/8 teaspoon unflavored gelatin powder or agar powder dissolved in cold broth or stock before heating
- 1 cup boiling water plus 1 reduced-sodium chicken bouillon cube, or 1 envelope instant chicken broth or granules, or 1/2 to 3/4 teaspoon chicken extract or soup base, or 2 teaspoons vegetarian-based chicken broth powder

BROTH, CHICKEN OR BEEF, FAT-FREE – 1 can
- ⊢ 1 can regular broth, refrigerated in the container for 8 to 12 hours (or in the freezer for 20 to 30 minutes) before removing solidified fat from the top

BROTH, VEGETABLE – 1 cup
- ⊢ 1 cup boiling water plus one of the following: instant vegetable broth package, vegetable bouillon cube, no-salt vegan vegetable cube, or 1/2 to 3/4 teaspoon powdered or jarred vegetable or mushroom soup base
- ⊢ 1 cup bean or vegetable cooking water (water left from cooking beans or mild-tasting vegetables)
- ⊢ 1 cup mushroom soaking water (from dried mushrooms rehydrated with boiling water)

BROWN RICE FLOUR See RICE FLOUR, BROWN

BROWN RICE SYRUP/YINNIE (Chinese naturally processed sweetener) – 1 cup See also JAPANESE BLACK SUGAR SYRUP
- ⊢ 3/4 cup mild-flavored liquid honey or maple syrup plus 2 tablespoons water
- ⊢ 1 cup agave syrup/nectar or coconut nectar

BROWN RICE VINEGAR See JAPANESE BROWN RICE VINEGAR/ GENMAIZU

BUDDHA'S HAND/FINGERED CITRON – 1
- ⊢ 1 fresh etrog citron or pomelo
- ⊢ 2 large, thick-skinned lemons

BULLWHIP KELP, DRIED (brown algae) – 1 ounce
- ⊢ 1 ounce dried wakame or alaria/winged kelp

BURDOCK ROOT/GOBO/VETOING (Japanese root vegetable) – 2 ounces (6-inch piece/1/2 cup scraped and sliced)

- 1/2 cup thawed frozen burdock strips or canned burdock pieces, rinsed in cold water
- 1/3 cup dried shaved burdock root/*gobo*, soaked in warm water until softened
- 1/2 cup wild burdock root/lesser burdock/*Arctium minus*
- 1/2 cup peeled and sliced white salsify/oyster plant or black salsify/scorzonera (less sweet)
- 1 medium parsnip or White Satin carrot, peeled and sliced on the bias (sweeter)

C

CALAMANSI *See CALAMONDIN*

CALAMONDIN/KALAMANSI/LIMAU KETSURI (Southeast Asian citrus fruit) – 1
- ⇛ 3 large kumquats or mandarinquats
- ⇛ 2 or 3 fully ripe Key limes
- ⇛ 1 small blood orange

CALAMONDIN JUICE, fresh or frozen – 1 tablespoon
- ⇛ 2 teaspoons lemon or lime juice plus 1 teaspoon tangerine or mandarin juice (or orange juice)
- ⇛ 1 teaspoon presweetened calamansi concentrate plus 2 teaspoons water (will add sweetness)

CANDLE NUTS/KEMIR NUTS/BIJI KEMIRI (Southeast Asian thickening agent) – 1/4 cup
- ⇛ 1/4 cup Macadamia nuts, cashews, or Brazil nuts

CANE VINEGAR, WHITE/SUKANG MAASIM (Filipino mild, all-purpose sugarcane vinegar) – 1 tablespoon
- ⇛ 1 tablespoon unseasoned rice vinegar or rice wine vinegar
- ⇛ 1 scant tablespoon distilled white vinegar

CARAMEL SYRUP/NUOC MAU (Vietnamese sweetener) – 1 teaspoon
- ⇛ 1 1/2 teaspoons granulated sugar

CARDAMOM PODS, BLACK/BROWN/CHA KOH/TSAO-KO; THAO QUA – 1 tablespoon
- ⇛ 1 tablespoon Chinese cardamom/*Amomum globosum* (less expensive; more pungent)

☞ 2 or 3 whole cloves

CASHEWS/YAO DOU/KAJU/CASOY – 1 cup:
☞ 1 cup macadamia or pine nuts
☞ 1 cup almonds (less soft)

CASHEWS, FRESH – 1 cup:
☞ 1 cup raw cashews soaked in 2 cups cold water for 10 to 12 hours

CASHEW WINE VINEGAR/GOAN VINEGAR – 1 tablespoon:
☞ 1 tablespoon cider vinegar

CASSIA See CINNAMON, GROUND (Chinese, Indonesian, Korintje, Padang, cassia)

CASSIA BARK See CINNAMON STICK, INDONESIAN KORINTJE

CASSIA LEAF/CINNAMON LEAF/TEJ PATTA (Indian flavoring agent) – 1 dried leaf
☞ 1 whole clove or small pinch ground cloves
☞ 1 small dried Turkish bay leaf and a few grains cassia cinnamon

CAYENNE CHILI, FRESH (green or red) – 1
☞ 1 to 3 fresh green or red serrano or Thai chilis, depending on size
☞ 1/4 to 1/2 teaspoon ground cayenne pepper or paste

CAYENNE PEPPER, GROUND/GROUND RED PEPPER – 1/2 teaspoon
☞ 1/2 teaspoon Aleppo, de árbol, or Thai chili powder
☞ 1/2 teaspoon hot paprika
☞ 3/4 teaspoon crushed red pepper flakes
☞ 3 to 4 drops hot pepper sauce, such as Tabasco or Crystal

CELLOPHANE NOODLES, See NOODLES, CELLOPHANE

CELTUCE See TAIWANESE LETTUCE

CHAI SEASONING/YOGI TEA (Thai and Indian spice mix for tea) – 2 teaspoons
- 1 teaspoon ground cardamom plus 1/4 teaspoon each ground allspice, ground cinnamon, ground ginger, and ground nutmeg
- 1-inch cinnamon stick, 2 green cardamom pods, and 3 whole cloves

CHAPATI/CHAPATTI (Indian unleavened whole-wheat bread) – 1
- 1 whole-wheat tortilla or pita bread

CHAPATI FLOUR See ATTA/PATENT DURA FLOUR/CHAPATI FLOUR

CHAROLI NUTS/CHIRONGI/CALUMPANG (Indian sweetmeat garnish) – 1 ounce
- 1 ounce slivered blanched almonds
- 1 ounce chopped unsalted pistachios or hazelnuts

CHAR SIU SAUCE See CHINESE BARBECUE SAUCE

CHEE HOU SAUCE/CHU HOU PASTE (Chinese braising sauce) – 1/4 cup
- 1/4 cup hoisin sauce diluted with a little rice vinegar (less spicy)

CHENNA/SOFT PANEER (Indian soft fresh cheese) – 4 ounces See also PANEER
- 4 ounces drained ricotta cheese (drained 8 to 12 hours in a dampened, cheesecloth-lined sieve set over a bowl in the refrigerator)
- 4 ounces dry curd cottage cheese
- 4 ounces paneer (firmer texture)

CHERIMOYA/CUSTARD APPLE, FRESH (sweet tropical fruit) – 1
- 8 ounces thawed frozen cherimoya pulp
- 1 fresh atemoya, soursop/guanabana, sweetsop, or mango

CHESTNUTS, FRESH SHELLED/KURI/BAM – 1 cup
- 1 cup frozen, canned, or packaged chestnuts

- 1/2 cup (3 ounces) dried chestnuts soaked in 1 cup hot water 4 hours, or in cold water 8 to 12 hours
- 1 cup shelled hazelnuts, macadamia nuts, or chufa nuts
- 1 cup large cooked chickpeas, or drained and rinsed canned chickpeas
- 1 cup breadfruit seeds
- 1 cup shelled, leached, and dried acorns, preferably white oak or valley oak

CHICKPEA FLOUR/CHANA BESAN, TOASTED (South Asian thickening agent) – 1 cup

- 1 cup toasted rice powder

Make Your Own Toast 1 cup chickpea flour in a dry heavy skillet over medium heat until golden, about 10 minutes, stirring constantly; or roast on a baking sheet in a preheated 350°F oven until golden, 12 to 15 minutes, stirring once. Store, tightly sealed, in a cool, dark place.

CHICKPEAS/CHANNA, DRIED – 1 cup

- 2 cups thawed frozen green garbanzos (smaller; higher in protein)
- 1 cup dried Italian thin-skinned chickpeas/*ceci flora* (smaller; thinner skinned; more tender)
- 1 cup dried black chickpeas/*kala chana,* or black organic kabuli chickpeas (smaller; brownish-black; thick-skinned)
- 1 cup dried Turkish skinned chickpeas (less flavorful; saves time)
- 1 cup dried tan or white tepary beans (larger)

CHILI BEAN SAUCE/TOBAN JIANG/DOUBAN JIANG (Chinese condiment) – 2 generous tablespoons

- 2 tablespoons black bean sauce (or black bean and garlic sauce) plus a little chili oil, hot pepper sauce, or chopped hot chili
- 1 tablespoon chili bean paste mixed with 1 crushed garlic clove and 2 teaspoons each soy sauce and rice vinegar

CHILI GARLIC SAUCE/LA JIAO JIANG (Chinese condiment) – 1 tablespoon

- 1 tablespoon Chinese chili sauce or sambal oelek, plus minced fresh garlic

- 1 teaspoon crushed red pepper flakes plus few grains granulated garlic
- 2 teaspoons Chinese chili oil

Make Your Own Process in a food processor 5 (3-inch) fresh, chopped, seeded red chilis, 3 garlic cloves, and 2 tablespoons seasoned rice vinegar. Store, refrigerated, up to 1 week.

CHILI OIL, CHINESE/DAU OT/LA JIAO YOU (dipping sauce and cooking condiment) – 1 teaspoon

- 1 teaspoon Asian sesame oil (or peanut oil) plus 1/8 teaspoon ground cayenne pepper or hot chili powder
- 1/8 teaspoon (or more) crushed red pepper flakes or hot sauce, such as Tabasco or Crystal
- 1 teaspoon Thai or Malaysian chili oil (more pungent)

Make Your Own Slowly heat 1/2 cup peanut or sesame oil and 2 tablespoons crushed red pepper flakes until the oil becomes a shade darker, about 5 minutes (or microwave in a 2-cup glass measuring jug for 1 minute). Let sit, covered, for 24 hours, then strain through a fine-mesh sieve; discard the pepper flakes and store the oil for up to 6 months in the refrigerator. Makes about 1/2 cup.

CHILI SOY SAUCE – 1 cup

- 3/4 cup light soy sauce, and 3 tablespoons Chinese chili sauce
- 3/4 cup light soy sauce, 1/4 cup deveined and seeded minced fresh chilis, plus sugar to taste (Wear plastic gloves when handling chilis and avoid touching your face.)

CHILI THREADS, DRIED RED See KOREAN RED PEPPER THREADS

CHILI VINEGAR (Indian condiment) – 1 cup

Make Your Own Chop 5 or 6 hot dried red chilis and place in a sterilized jar with 1 cup cider vinegar. Cover and let sit in a cool, dark place for 7 to 10 days, shaking the bottle occasionally. Strain and discard the chilis. Store in an airtight container in a cool, dry place; it will keep for up to 6 months.

CHINESE ARTICHOKE *See CROSNES/CHINESE ARTICHOKE/CHOROGI*

CHINESE BABY BROCCOLI/GAI LAN MIEW – 1 pound
- 1 pound regular Chinese broccoli with stems thinly sliced

CHINESE BARBECUE SAUCE/CHAR SIU CHIANG – 1 cup
- 1 cup oyster sauce
- 1 cup vegetarian barbecue sauce, such as AGV or Bull Head brand

CHINESE BLACK BEAN GARLIC SAUCE *See BLACK BEAN GARLIC SAUCE*

CHINESE BLACK BEAN SAUCE *See BLACK BEAN SAUCE*

CHINESE BLACK BEANS, FERMENTED *See FERMENTED BLACK BEANS*

CHINESE BLACK FUNGUS *See CLOUD EAR/BLACK TREE FUNGUS*

CHINESE BLACK MUSHROOM, DRIED/GAN XIANG GU *See SHIITAKE MUSHROOMS*

CHINESE BLACK RICE VINEGAR/CHINKIANG/SHANXI/HEI MI CU – 1 tablespoon
- 1 1/2 teaspoons each non-aged balsamic vinegar and red wine vinegar
- 1 tablespoon cider or unseasoned red rice vinegar plus 1 or 2 drops Worcestershire sauce

CHINESE BROCCOLI/CHINESE KALE/GAI LAN/JIE LAN/KAI LAN – 1 pound
- 1 pound Chinese baby broccoli/*gai lan miew* (smaller, slimmer stemmed)
- 1 pound broccoli raab/rabe, or *yau choy/yai tsoi* (stronger flavor)
- 1 pound broccolini, or stalks of regular broccoli sliced lengthwise
- 1 pound field mustard flower bud stems/*Brassica rapa*

CHINESE BROWN BEAN PASTE See CHINESE YELLOW/BROWN BEAN SAUCE

CHINESE CABBAGE/CHINESE LEAVES/NAPA CABBAGE/HAKUSAI – 1 pound
- 1 pound Tenderheart cabbage or Savoy cabbage
- 1 pound bok choy, choy sum, green chard, frilly-leafed collard greens, or curly green kale (for cooked dishes)
- 1 pound torn or shredded romaine lettuce; or plain-leaved Russian kale, massaged with salt and olive oil (for salads and cold dishes)

CHINESE CELERY/ASIAN CELERY/NAN LING CELERY/PARCEL/KUN CHOY – 1 cup chopped
- 1 cup chopped lovage stalks and leaves
- 1 cup chopped celery hearts (or thin, tender celery stalks and tops) plus some flat-leaf parsley
- 1 cup Mitsuba, or celery leaves plus a little chopped flat-leaf parsley (to replace Chinese celery leaves)

CHINESE CHEE HOU/CHOU HEE SAUCE See CHEE HOU SAUCE

CHINESE CHILI BEAN PASTE See SICHUAN CHILI BEAN PASTE

CHINESE CHILI BEAN SAUCE See CHILI BEAN SAUCE

CHINESE CHILI, DRIED/GAN LA JIAO – 1/4 cup
- 1/4 cup cayenne, de árbol, or Thai chilis

CHINESE CHILI FLAKES/LA JIAO MIAN – 1 tablespoon
- 1 tablespoon Korean coarse chili flakes/*gochugaru*
- 1 1/2 teaspoons Italian crushed red pepper flakes

CHINESE CHILI-GARLIC SAUCE See CHILI-GARLIC SAUCE

CHINESE CHILI OIL See CHILI OIL, CHINESE

CHINESE CHIVES/CHINESE LEEK See GARLIC CHIVES

CHINESE COOKING WINE/LIAO JIU See CHINESE YELLOW RICE COOKING WINE

CHINESE CURRY POWDER – 1 teaspoon
- 1 teaspoon mild Madras curry powder
- 1/4 teaspoon each ground turmeric, cardamom, ginger, and cumin

CHINESE DATES See JUJUBES/NATSUME

CHINESE DIPPING SAUCE – 1 cup
- 1/2 cup each soy sauce and brown rice vinegar plus 1 teaspoon grated fresh ginger (or chili oil)

Make Your Own Stir together 1/2 cup soy sauce, 1/4 cup water, 2 tablespoons seasoned rice vinegar, and 2 teaspoons sugar until the sugar dissolves. Add 2 tablespoons thinly sliced scallions or green onions, if desired.

CHINESE DRIED SCALLOP/GAN BEI/CONPOY (flavoring agent) – 1 ounce
- 1 ounce tuna bottarga/*bottarga di tonno*
- 1 or 2 tablespoons clam juice (for the flavor)

CHINESE DUCK SAUCE See PLUM SAUCE

CHINESE DUMPLING DOUGH – 8 ounces
- 8 ounces refrigerated buttermilk biscuit dough

CHINESE DUMPLING WRAPPERS/SIU KOW – 1 pound
- 1 pound wonton wrappers

CHINESE EGG NOODLES/CHOW MEIN NOODLES/MEE/BAH-MI/MIAN TIAO, FRESH – 1 pound See also CHINESE WHEAT NOODLES
- 1 pound fresh Chinese wheat noodles or ramen noodles

☞ 12 ounces dried spaghetti or fettuccine (longer cooking time)

CHINESE FERMENTED BLACK BEANS *See FERMENTED BLACK BEANS*

CHINESE FISH SAUCE/FISH MIST/YUE LO *See FISH SAUCE*

CHINESE FIVE-SPICE POWDER – 1 teaspoon
- ☞ 1/8 teaspoon each ground cinnamon, ground cloves, ground ginger, ground Sichuan pepper (or freshly ground black or white pepper), and ground star anise (or crushed anise or fennel seed)
- ☞ 1 whole ground star anise (or 1/2 teaspoon star anise powder) plus a touch of ground white pepper or ginger
- ☞ 1/2 teaspoon anise or fennel seeds, crushed, plus a touch of ground white pepper or ginger

CHINESE FLOWERING CABBAGE *See CHOY SUM*

CHINESE FLOWERING QUINCE *See FLOWERING QUINCE*

CHINESE GARLIC STEMS/SUAN TAI – 4 ounces
- ☞ 4 ounces garlic chives, or garlic scapes (curly garlic shoots)
- ☞ 4 ounces green onions plus a little chopped garlic
- ☞ 4 ounces unsprayed wild garlic greens/shoots/onion grass/*Allium vineale*

CHINESE GINGER *See FINGERROOT*

CHINESE HAM (Yunnan or Jinhua) – 1 pound
- ☞ 1 pound smoky Serrano ham,
- ☞ 1 pound dry-cured and smoked country-style ham, such as Smithfield (request a center cut, 1 inch thick)
- ☞ 1 pound Westphalian ham
- ☞ 1 pound prosciutto

CHINESE HOISIN SAUCE *See HOISIN SAUCE*

CHINESE HOT PEPPER OIL See CHILI OIL, CHINESE

CHINESE HOT RED CHILI See CHINESE CHILI, DRIED

CHINESE KALE See CHINESE BROCCOLI

CHINESE KEYS See FINGERROOT

CHINESE LEAF LETTUCE/PAK KAD/SANG CHOY
   ⇨ Romaine/cos lettuce

CHINESE MU SHU SAUCE See MU SHU SAUCE

CHINESE MUSTARD See MUSTARD, CHINESE

CHINESE MUSTARD CABBAGE /GAI CHOY/TAKANA – 1 pound See also MUSTARD GREENS
   ⇨ 1 pound mustard greens; turnip greens; or escarole, especially the dark outer leaves
   ⇨ 1 pound Japanese mustard spinach/*Komatsu-na* (smaller, darker-colored leaves)
   ⇨ 1 pound Chinese spinach/*yin choy* or mature curly-leaf spinach/Savoy (milder flavor)

CHINESE NOODLES See CHINESE EGG NOODLES; CHINESE WHEAT NOODLES

CHINESE OKRA/ANGLED LOOFAH SQUASH/SILK SQUASH/SING GWA/ HECHIMA, FRESH – 1 pound (2 medium)
   ⇨ 1 pound young sponge gourd or medium zucchini (peeling unnecessary)
   ⇨ 1 large English/hothouse cucumber (peeled and any seeds removed)

CHINESE PANCAKES See MOO SHU PANCAKES

CHINESE PARSLEY/FRESH CORIANDER See CILANTRO

CHINESE PEPPER See SICHUAN PEPPER

CHINESE PICKLED GARLIC – 1 cup
Make Your Own Separate and peel the cloves from 5 heads (about 8 ounces) of garlic. Heat with 1/2 cup unseasoned rice vinegar, 1 tablespoon sugar, and 1/2 teaspoon salt until boiling; let cool. Refrigerate in a covered jar for at least 1 month before using.

CHINESE PRESERVED CABBAGE/SALTED MUSTARD CABBAGE/TIAN JIN/TUNG TSAI – 1 tablespoon
  ⊳ 1 tablespoon sauerkraut or napa cabbage kimchi (milder)

CHINESE PRESERVING MELON See SQUASH, ASIAN

CHINESE RADISH See DAIKON

CHINESE RED DATES See JUJUBES/NATSUME

CHINESE RED RICE POWDER/HONG QU FEN (coloring agent) – 1 tablespoon
  ⊳ 1 tablespoon red rice (labeled red yeast rice) ground to a fine powder in a spice/coffee grinder

CHINESE RED RICE VINEGAR/DA HONG ZHE CU (vinegar dipping/ condiment sauce) – 1 tablespoon
  ⊳ 1 tablespoon Japanese rice vinegar (milder)
  ⊳ 1 tablespoon red wine vinegar sweetened with a little sugar
  ⊳ 1 tablespoon Chinese black rice vinegar or cider vinegar

CHINESE RED SPINACH/YIN TSAI See AMARANTH GREENS

CHINESE RICE FLOUR See RICE FLOUR, CHINESE

CHINESE RICE WINE/HUANG JIN/CHIEW *See SHAOXING*

CHINESE SAUSAGE/LAP CHEONG (thin cured sweet seasoned sausage) – 1 pound
- 1 pound chorizo de Bilbao or another Spanish dry-cured chorizo
- 1 pound Portuguese dry-cured chouriço or linguiça
- 1 pound Italian pepperoni or dry salami

CHINESE SESAME PASTE *See SESAME PASTE*

CHINESE SHANXI VINEGAR *See CHINESE BLACK RICE VINEGAR*

CHINESE SHRIMP PASTE/XIA JIANG *See SHRIMP PASTE, FERMENTED*

CHINESE SHRIMP SAUCE/BALICHAO *See SHRIMP SAUCE, FERMENTED*

CHINESE SOY SAUCE *See SOY SAUCE, CHINESE DARK; SOY SAUCE, CHINESE DOUBLE DARK; SOY SAUCE, CHINESE LIGHT*

CHINESE STEAMED BUNS/MANTOU – 1 dozen
- 1 dozen unbaked refrigerated biscuits, such as Pillsbury buttermilk, flattened slightly, folded in half, and steamed until doubled in size, about 10 minutes

CHINESE SUGAR *See SUGAR, BROWN ROCK; SUGAR, YELLOW/CLEAR ROCK*

CHINESE SWEET-AND-SOUR SAUCE – 1/2 cup
- 1/2 cup Italian sweet and sour sauce/*agrodolce*
Make Your Own Simmer 1/4 cup each plum jam and apricot (or peach) jam with 1/4 cup cider vinegar until slightly thickened, about 10 minutes (or microwave on High for 4 minutes); let cool. The sauce will thicken further as it cools.

CHINESE SWEET BEAN PASTE/SAUCE See SICHUAN SWEET BEAN PASTE

CHINESE TURNIP See DAIKON

CHINESE VEGETABLE MARROW See SQUASH, ASIAN

CHINESE WATERCRESS/ONG CHOY – 4 ounces
- 4 ounces watercress, garden/pepper cress, or upland cress

CHINESE WHEAT NOODLES/SHANDONG LA MIAN/HOKKIEN MEE, FRESH – 1 pound See also CHINESE EGG NOODLES; NOODLES, CELLOPHANE
- 1 pound fresh Chinese egg noodles or fresh-frozen ramen noodles
- 12 ounces dried thin Japanese wheat noodles/*hiyamugi/somen*, Korean thin wheat noodles/*somyun/gougsou*, or Filipino fine white wheat noodles/*miswa*
- 12 ounces dried spaghettini or vermicelli

CHINESE WHITE RICE VINEGAR/CLEAR RICE VINEGAR/BAI MI CU – 1/2 cup
- 1/3 cup distilled white vinegar or cider vinegar plus 3 tablespoons water

CHINESE YELLOW/BROWN BEAN SAUCE/HUGAN JIANG – 1 tablespoon
- 1 tablespoon canned, salted yellow beans, rinsed briefly in a fine sieve, then mashed with a fork
- 1 tablespoon Japanese all-purpose light miso, such as *shinshu*

CHINESE YELLOW RICE COOKING WINE/MICHIU/MI JIU – 1 tablespoon
- 1 tablespoon pure yellow rice wine/*huang jiu,* such as Shaoxing, plus a few grains of salt
- 1 tablespoon glutinous yellow rice wine/*gnow mei dew*

⊨ 1 tablespoon sake, dry vermouth, Latin American *vino seco*, or medium dry sherry such as amontillado

CHIVES, FRESH, FROZEN, OR FREEZE DRIED – 4 ounces
⊨ 4 ounces green parts of scallions or green onions, smashed and cut lengthwise into ribbons
⊨ 4 ounces garlic chives or Chinese garlic stems (more garlicky tasting)
⊨ 4 ounces garlic leaves, slivered (cut leaves sparingly when the plants are no more than 8 inches tall)
⊨ 4 ounces Egyptian walking onion leaves, slivered
⊨ 4 ounces unsprayed wild garlic foliage/shoots/*Allium vineale*

CHORIZO DE BILBAO (Filipino spicy cured sausage) – 1 pound
⊨ 1 pound Csabai or Gyulai Hungarian smoked sausage
⊨ 1 pound spicy smoked kiebasa

CHOY SUM/YU CHOY (Chinese flowering cabbage) – 1 pound
⊨ 1 pound baby bok choy, Chinese baby broccoli/*gai lan miew*, or Chinese broccoli

CHRYSANTHEMUM LEAVES, EDIBLE/GARLAND CHRYSANTHEMUM/ SHUNGIKU/ TUNG HO/ SUKGOT/KIKUNA (slightly bitter greens) – 1 pound
⊨ 1 pound mature arugula, young dandelion leaves, watercress, or escarole

CILANTRO/FRESH CORIANDER LEAVES/CHINESE PARSLEY/DHANIA/ KOTHMIR – 1 tablespoon chopped leaves
⊨ 1 teaspoon dried broken leaf cilantro,
⊨ 1 tablespoon chopped fresh sawleaf herb/*culantro*
⊨ 1 tablespoon chopped Italian flat-leaf parsley leaves, 1/8 teaspoon sage, and 1/8 teaspoon finely grated lime or lemon zest
⊨ 1 tablespoon chopped Italian flat-leaf parsley sprigs (for color)
⊨ Small piece cilantro-flavored mini bouillon cube (for soups or stews; reduce the salt in the recipe accordingly)

CILANTRO, MICRO – 1 ounce
- ᴵ 1 ounce cilantro leaves, amaranth sprouts, or watercress

CILANTRO ROOT *See CORIANDER ROOT*

CINNAMON STICK, INDONESIAN KORINTJE – 1 (3- or 4-inch) stick
- ᴵ 1 (5-inch) soft Ceylon cinnamon stick/canela
- ᴵ 2 teaspoons ground cinnamon (to replace a smashed/crushed cinnamon stick used in cooking)
- ᴵ 1/4 teaspoon ground cinnamon (to replace a whole cinnamon stick removed after cooking)
- ᴵ 1 tablespoon cinnamon chunks (to flavor coffee, mulled wine, or cider)

CINNAMON, GROUND (Ceylon, Sri Lanka, Mexican, canela) – 1 teaspoon
- ᴵ 1-inch Ceylon/Sri Lanka cinnamon stick, crumbled or grated with a Microplane grater
- ᴵ 2/3 teaspoon Indonesia/Korintje or China cassia cinnamon
- ᴵ 1/4 to 1/2 teaspoon Vietnamese/Saigon cassia cinnamon

CINNAMON, GROUND (Chinese, Indonesian, Korintje, Padang, cassia) – 1 teaspoon
- ᴵ 1 1/2 teaspoons pure Ceylon/Sri Lanka cinnamon/canela
- ᴵ 1/4 teaspoon cinnamon extract
- ᴵ 1/2 teaspoon ground allspice plus scant 1/8 teaspoon ground nutmeg
- ᴵ 1/4 teaspoon ground cardamom plus 1/8 teaspoon ground nutmeg
- ᴵ 1 teaspoon apple or pumpkin pie spice

CINNAMON, GROUND (Vietnamese/Saigon cassia/cassia Loureiro) – 1 teaspoon
- ᴵ 1 1/4 teaspoons Indonesia/Korintje or China/Tung Hing cassia cinnamon
- ᴵ 2 teaspoons pure Ceylon/Sri Lanka cinnamon/canela/*cinnamomum zeylanicum/verum*

CINNAMON, SOFT-QUILL See CINNAMON, GROUND (Ceylon, Sri Lanka, Mexican, canela)

CITRON/YUJA (Asian large tart citrus) – 1 fruit
↪ 1 large lemon (juice and zest only; not the white pith)

CITRUS SOY SAUCE/TOYOMANSI See SOY SAUCE, FILIPINO CITRUS

CLOUD EAR/BLACK TREE FUNGUS/HED HUNA/YUN'ER/WUN YEE (dried Asian mushroom) – 1/2 ounce (1/4 to 1/3 cup)
↪ 1/2 ounce dried wood ear fungus/*mook yee/hei mu er/kikurage* (larger, thicker, tougher; increase the cooking time)
↪ 1/2 ounce dried silver ear/white fungus/*sit gnee/yin'er/nam trang* (white to pale gold)
↪ 1/2 ounce small dried shiitake mushrooms (triple the soaking time)

COCONUT BUTTER/CREAMED COCONUT – 1 cup for cooking
↪ 1 cup vegetable shortening or unsalted butter (lacks coconut flavor)
Make Your Own Process 4 cups dried unsweetened flaked or desiccated coconut in a food processor or high-speed blender until reduced to a paste, 15 to 20 minutes, scraping down the sides of the bowl as needed. Store in a lidded jar at room temperature up to 2 months.

COCONUT CHIPS
Make Your Own Slice fresh coconut into wafer-thin strips, sprinkle with salt (optional), spread out on baking pans, and bake at 325°F until crisp, 25 to 30 minutes, rotating the pans and flipping the chips halfway through. Cool and store in an airtight container. (Freezing the whole coconut overnight makes shelling it easier.)

COCONUT CREAM, UNSWEETENED – 1/2 cup
↪ 1/2 cup thick liquid that rises to the top of canned or homemade coconut milk after chilling it several hours
↪ 1 (13.5-ounce) can coconut milk simmered until reduced to 1/2 cup, 40 to 45 minutes

‣ 1/2 cup heavy cream plus 1/4 teaspoon coconut extract

COCONUT MILK, FRESH – 1 cup
‣ 3 tablespoons canned cream of coconut plus enough water to make 1 cup

COCONUT MILK, FULL-FAT CANNED (53 to 55 % coconut extract) – 1 cup for cooking
‣ 1/4 cup (one-third of a packet) concentrated coconut cream mixed with 3/4 cup water
‣ 1/2 cup unsweetened coconut cream mixed with 1/2 cup water (whisk or stir the coconut milk before measuring)
‣ 1 cup coconut powder mixed with 1 cup water
‣ 1 cup half-and-half plus 1/2 teaspoon coconut extract (optional)
‣ 1 cup thin cauliflower puree plus 1/2 teaspoon coconut extract

Make Your Own Pour 1 1/4 cups boiling water over 1 cup packed fresh or frozen grated/shredded coconut (or unsweetened dried coconut); cool to room temperature. Process in a high-powered blender until smooth, about 2 minutes, then strain in a nutmilk bag or cheesecloth-lined sieve, pressing on the pulp to extract all the liquid. For light/lite coconut milk that resists curdling when heated, pour 1 cup water through the same puréed coconut and press again. To prevent full-fat coconut milk from curdling, add a scant 1/8 teaspoon baking soda before heating.

COCONUT MILK, LIGHT/LITE CANNED – 1 cup
‣ 1 cup of the second pressing of fresh grated coconut after making homemade coconut milk
‣ 1 cup lowfat or nonfat milk plus 1/2 teaspoon coconut extract
‣ 7/8 cup fresh coconut water plus 2 tablespoons full-fat sour cream or regular coconut milk
‣ 3/4 cup canned or homemade coconut milk mixed with 1/4 cup water
‣ 1/2 cup canned or homemade coconut milk mixed with 1/2 cup soymilk

☞ 1/3 cup unsweetened coconut cream mixed with 2/3 cup water

☞ 1 cup prepared potato milk, such as DariFree; or lactose-free milk, such as Lactaid (for coconut-free cooking; not for whipped topping)

COCONUT NECTAR/PALM SYRUP/EVAPORATED COCONUT SAP/ KITHUL TREACLE (thick, dark sweetener) – 1 cup

☞ 1 cup dark agave syrup/nectar, birch syrup, brown rice syrup, maple syrup, or *yacón* syrup

☞ 3/4 cup liquid honey plus 2 tablespoons water

COCONUT OIL, REFINED – 1 cup

☞ 1 cup firm rendered leaf lard

☞ 1 cup solid shortening

☞ 1 cup liquid and pourable coconut oil, or neutral-flavored vegetable oil, such as canola

COCONUT PALM SUGAR, GRANULATED See PALM SUGAR, LIGHT

COCONUT VINEGAR/SUKANG TUBA/NAM SOM MAPLOW (Filipino low-acidity vinegar) – 1/3 cup

☞ 1/3 cup organic coconut vinegar (sold in health food stores)

☞ 1/3 cup white sugarcane vinegar/*sukang maasim*

☞ 3 tablespoons cider vinegar plus 2 tablespoons water

☞ 1/4 cup rice vinegar plus 1 tablespoon water

COCONUT WATER/JUICE – 1 1/2 cups (contents of one young, fresh coconut)

☞ 1/2 cup canned coconut milk blended with 1 cup plain water

COLTSFOOT, SWEET/BUTTERBUR/FUKINOTO/KUAN DONG HUA (stalk vegetable) – 1 pound

☞ 1 pound canned butterbur stalks packed in water

☞ 1 pound thick celery stalks

CORIANDER ROOT/RAK PAK CHI/PAK CHEE MET (Thai seasoning) – 3 medium (1 tablespoon chopped)
- ☞ 3 tablespoons minced cilantro stems

CORIANDER SEED, DRIED/DHANIA (Indian spice) – 1 tablespoon (1/8 ounce)
- ☞ 1 to 1 1/2 teaspoons ground coriander
- ☞ 2 tablespoons fresh green coriander seeds
- ☞ 1 tablespoon caraway or fennel seeds
- ☞ 1 1/2 teaspoons black cardamom seeds or cumin seeds

CROSNES/CHINESE ARTICHOKE/CHOROGI (small crunchy tubers) – 1 pound (2 cups)
- ☞ 1 pound chopped sunchokes/Jerusalem artichokes, salsify, artichoke hearts, or young burdock root (Place the cut vegetables in acidulated water to keep them from discoloring.)

CUKA See INDONESIAN VINEGAR

CULANTRO/FITWEED/RECAO/NGO GAI/PAK CHI FARANG (Southeast Asian seasoning) – 1 fresh leaf
- ☞ 1 teaspoon each fresh minced cilantro, mint, and basil leaves
- ☞ 1 large sprig fresh cilantro or 1 scant tablespoon minced (less flavorful)

CUMIN SEEDS, BLACK/KALA JEER/ZEERA (Thai and Indian seasoning) – 1 teaspoon
- ☞ 1 teaspoon amber or white cumin seeds (less flavorful)
- ☞ 1/2 teaspoon toasted ground cumin seeds
- ☞ 1/2 teaspoon coriander seeds or caraway seeds

CURRY LEAF/DAUN KARI/KARI PATTA/KARAPINCHA/KITHA NEEM/ BAI KAREE (South Asian seasoning) – 1 fresh sprig (8 to 12 leaves)
- ☞ 12 to 16 dried or semidried curry leaves (check for aroma; dried leaves can have little flavor)
- ☞ 1 teaspoon curry leaf/kari patta powder

- 2 dried salam leaves/*daun salam*
- 2 to 3 dried bay leaves
- 1 tablespoon chopped fresh cilantro leaves (grassier flavor)

CURRY OIL (Indian seasoning) – 1/2 cup
Make Your Own Gently heat 1/2 cup peanut or vegetable oil and 1 tablespoon mild Indian curry powder or paste for 15 minutes (do not let the oil get too hot). Cool, then strain through a small cloth-lined sieve; store, refrigerated, for up to 3 months. Or, rather than heating the oil, dry-toast the curry powder, then mix to a paste with 1 tablespoon of the oil; add the rest of the oil and shake to mix thoroughly; leave at room temperature for 8 to 12 hours, then strain.

CURRY PASTE, JUNGLE (Thai seasoning) – 1 tablespoon
- 1 tablespoon Thai Green Curry Paste

CURRY POWDER, JAPANESE/KARĒ POWDER. – 1 tablespoon
- 1 tablespoon Indian-style spice blend, such as S&B Oriental Curry Powder

CURRY POWDER, MADRAS – 1 tablespoon
- 1 tablespoon sweet or mild curry powder plus 1/16 teaspoon ground cayenne pepper

CURRY POWDER/SEASONING, VINDALOO – 1 tablespoon
- 1 tablespoon Vindaloo curry paste
- 2 teaspoons mild/regular sweet curry powder, 3/4 teaspoon hot paprika, and 1/4 teaspoon ground black pepper
- 1 tablespoon Madras curry powder plus 1/2 to 1 teaspoon crushed red pepper flakes

CURRY POWDER, STANDARD/REGULAR BLEND – 1 tablespoon, or to taste
- 1 tablespoon Columbo curry powder (West Indian; mild)
- 1 tablespoon Maharajah-style curry powder, sweet curry powder, Korma curry paste, Tikka masala paste, Patak's paste, or tandoori powder or paste (Indian; mild)

- 1 tablespoon Vadouvan curry blend (French-Indian; delicate and mild; flavored with shallots and garlic)
- 1 tablespoon Massaman curry blend (Southern Thai; mild; similar to Malaysian and Indian but with a nuttier flavor)
- 1 tablespoon Madras curry powder (classic all-purpose curry powder, spicier and less bitter than most commercial versions; sometimes contains chickpea flour for less heat)
- 1 tablespoon hot Madras curry powder (regular Madras curry powder plus a pinch of ground cayenne pepper)
- 1 tablespoon Muchi curry powder (Indian; hot and spicy)
- 2 tablespoons Thai kari/yellow curry paste or Thai Massaman curry paste (mild sweet/spicy)
- 2 tablespoons Thai Panang curry paste (mellow and moderately hot; contains lemongrass and chilis)
- 2 teaspoons Thai red curry paste (medium-hot)
- 2 teaspoons Thai green or hot Madras green curry paste
- 1 1/2 to 2 teaspoons Vindaloo curry paste or powder/seasoning (Indian; spicy/tangy and hot)
- 4 teaspoons garam masala (Indian; warm spice blend; add at the end of cooking to heighten the flavor)

CURRY POWDER, VIETNAMESE/BOT CARY – 1 tablespoon
- 1 tablespoon mild or medium-hot Madras-style curry powder

CUTTLEFISH, FRESH – 1 pound
- 1 pound fresh squid or octopus (less tender)
- 8 to 12 ounces Chinese dried squid soaked in water with a little baking soda until softened (for using cooked; baking soda tenderizes the squid)

D

DAIDAI JUICE (Japanese bitter citrus fruit juice) – 1 tablespoon
  ☞ 1 tablespoon lemon or lime juice

DAIKON/ASIAN WHITE RADISH/MOOLI/LOBOK/LUOPO – 1 pound
  ☞ 1 pound Korean radish/*mu* or jícama (sweeter)
  ☞ 1 pound white icicle radish, red radish, or young, crisp turnip (for using raw or pickled)
  ☞ 1 pound Japanese giant turnip/*kabura* (for using cooked or pickled)
  ☞ 5 to 6 ounces sliced or shredded dried daikon/*kiriboshi daikon*, soaked in lukewarm water for 30 to 60 minutes, then squeezed dry (for using cooked or pickled)

DAIKON GREENS/YOUNG DAIKON LEAVES/MU CHONG – 8 ounces
  ☞ 8 ounces watercress, broadleaf cress, curly cress, or arugula

DAIKON LEAF/MATURE DAIKON LEAVES/SHEN LI HON (Taiwan) – 1 bunch
  ☞ 1 bunch Taiwan lettuce/*a choy*, mustard greens, or turnip greens

DAIKON SPROUTS/KAIWARE – 4 ounces
  ☞ 4 ounces sunflower sprouts
  ☞ 4 ounces pea or chickpea shoots

DASHI/ICHIBAN DASHI/NIBAN DASHI (Japanese fish stock and seasoning) – 1 cup
  ☞ 1/4 teaspoon instant dashi granules, such as *hon-dashi* or *dashi-no-moto*, dissolved in 1 cup hot water (*hon-dashi* contains salt; *dashi-no-moto* contains salt, and some contain MSG)

- 1/3 teaspoon liquid dashi concentrate, such as *katsuo dashi, tsuyu no moto,* or *shiro dashi,* dissolved in 1 cup hot water (contains a little salt)
- 1/3 teaspoon white soy sauce/*shiro shoyu* dissolved in 1 cup hot water
- 1 cup kelp stock (10 grams/1/3 ounce kombu soaked in 1 cup cold water for 8 to 12 hours)
- 1/2 cup each light vegetable and seafood stock
- 1 cup low-sodium or diluted chicken broth (if the recipe contains chicken)

DASHI CONCENTRATE/SHIRI DASHI – 1 tablespoon

- 1 tablespoon white soy sauce/*shir shoyu*

DASHI, VEGETARIAN/KOMBU DASHI/SHOJIN DASHI – 1 cup

- 2 to 3 small squares of kombu/kelp and 1 dried shiitake mushroom soaked in 1 cup cold water for 30 to 60 minutes, then simmered for 10 to 15 minutes
- 1 cup low-sodium vegetable stock

DASHIMA *See KOMBU*

DATE-PALM JAGGERY, LIQUID/JHOLA GUR (Indian sweetener) – 1/4 cup

- 1/4 cup coconut nectar or maple syrup
- 1/4 cup grated cane jaggery or other palm sugar
- 1/4 cup dark brown or maple sugar, moistened to a coarse paste with 1 teaspoon light molasses

DHANIA JEERA POWDER (Indian spice blend) – 1 tablespoon

- 2 teaspoons roasted ground coriander and 1 teaspoon roasted ground cumin

DIPPING SAUCE *See ASIAN DIPPING SAUCE; CHINESE DIPPING SAUCE; KOREAN SESAME DIPPING SAUCE; PEANUT DIPPING SAUCE; TEMPURA DIPPING SAUCE; NAM PRIK; VIETNAMESE DIPPING SAUCE*

DOENJANG See KOREAN SOYBEAN PASTE

DUCK FAT, RENDERED – 1 tablespoon
- 1 tablespoon rendered goose fat, pork fat, tallow, or leaf lard
- 1 tablespoon fruity olive oil, or 1 1/2 teaspoons each olive oil and unsalted butter

DUCK SAUCE/SUÀN MÉI JIÀNG (Chinese condiment) – 1/4 cup
- 1/4 cup plum sauce thinned with a little orange juice See PLUM SAUCE

DUCK, LONG ISLAND/PEKING – 1 pound
- 1 pound female Muscovy duck (darker and tastier meat)
- 1 pound farm-raised Mallard, or wild duck (richer-tasting and less fatty)
- 1 pound gosling/young goose
- 1 pound squab

DUMPLING DOUGH See CHINESE DUMPLING DOUGH

DUMPLING WRAPPERS See CHINESE DUMPLING WRAPPERS

E

EDAMAME, FRESH OR FROZEN (young green soybeans) – 1 pound
- ⇨ 1 pound fresh chickpeas in the pod (steam or boil the 1-inch pods, then eat the single chickpea like edamame)
- ⇨ 1 pound young fresh garden peas in the pod (steam or boil, then eat the peas like edamame)
- ⇨ 1 pound smaller, more immature fava beans in the pod (steam or grill, then eat the beans like edamame)

EDAMAME, SHELLED AND COOKED, FRESH OR FROZEN – 8 ounces
- ⇨ 8 ounces blanched and peeled small fava beans
- ⇨ 8 ounces cooked baby lima beans
- ⇨ 8 ounces cooked green peas
- ⇨ 8 ounces chopped cooked green beans

EGG ROLL WRAPPERS – 1 pound
- ⇨ 1 pound lumpia wrappers
- ⇨ 1 pound wonton or gyoza wrappers (smaller)
- ⇨ 1 pound empanada wrappers (round)
- ⇨ 1 pound thin fresh pasta sheets, cut to size
- ⇨ 1 pound Vietnamese spring roll wrappers, rice paper, or fresh or dried bean curd skins/yuba sheets, cut to size (thinner, more delicate; gluten-free)

Make Your Own Beat together 1 cup all-purpose flour, 2 cups water, and 2 eggs. Spoon 1 tablespoon batter at a time into a 6-inch nonstick skillet and cook over low to medium heat until set on both sides, making thin flexible pale pancakes. Cover with a damp cloth until ready to use.

EGGPLANT, THAI PEA/MAKHUA PHUONG (pea-size green eggplants) – 1 pound

- ☞ 1 pound Thai green apple eggplants/ (golf-ball size) cut into quarters (soak in acidulated water before adding to the dish)
- ☞ 1 pound long slender Japanese or Chinese eggplants cut into bite-size pieces
- ☞ 1 pound frozen peas (added toward the end of cooking)

ENO FRUIT SALT POWDER (Indian leavening agent) – 1 teaspoon

- ☞ 1 teaspoon baking soda

ENOKI MUSHROOM/SNOW PUFF/ENOKITAKE – 1 bunch (6 ounces)

- ☞ 4 ounces canned enoki mushrooms, drained
- ☞ 6 to 7 ounces fresh oyster/shimeji or white cap/button mushrooms

F

FATBACK/LIEMPO (fresh unsalted pork fat) – 4-ounces (1 cup finely chopped)
- 4 ounces fat trimmed from a pork roast (package and freeze until needed)
- 4 ounces Italian lardo, soaked in water to cover for 8 to 10 hours, then rinsed and blotted dry
- 4 ounces salt pork, slab bacon, or thick presliced bacon, blanched in boiling water for 40 to 60 seconds, then rinsed and blotted dry

FENNEL SEEDS, DRIED/SAUNF (Indian seasoning) – 1 teaspoon whole seeds
- 1 scant teaspoon mature wild black fennel seeds/*Foeniculum vulgare* (more intense flavor)
- 1 1/2 teaspoons fresh green fennel seeds or 1 tablespoon minced fresh fennel leaves
- 1/2 teaspoon ground fennel seeds
- 1 scant teaspoon anise seeds
- 3/4 teaspoon caraway or dill seeds

FENUGREEK LEAVES, DRIED/KASURI METHI (Indian and Pakistani seasoning) – 1 tablespoon
- 1 teaspoon fenugreek powder; or a small pinch ground roasted fenugreek seeds (for curries; sprinkle over the dish just before serving)

FENUGREEK POWDER (Indian and Pakistani seasoning) – 1 teaspoon
- 1 tablespoon dried fenugreek leaves crushed through a medium-mesh sieve; discard stem pieces

FENUGREEK SEEDS/METHI KA BEEJ/DAANA-METHI (Indian curry flavoring) – 1 tablespoon whole seeds
- ☞ 1 3/4 tablespoons ground fenugreek seeds
- ☞ 2 teaspoons brown mustard seeds and 1 teaspoon celery seeds

FERMENTED BLACK BEANS/FERMENTED BLACK SOYBEANS/DOW SEE/DOUCHI (Chinese seasoning) – 1 tablespoon
- ☞ 1 1/2 tablespoons fermented black bean paste/*douchi jiang*
- ☞ 1 to 2 tablespoons Japanese dark miso, such as *inaka* or *hatcho*
- ☞ 1 to 2 tablespoons mashed salt-packed capers
- ☞ 2 to 3 tablespoons dark soy sauce (usually labeled all-purpose)

FERMENTED BLACK GARLIC – 1 whole head/bulb (1/2 ounce)
- ☞ 1 well-roasted whole garlic head/bulb plus a little balsamic vinegar or molasses
- ☞ 1 to 1 1/2 teaspoons fermented black garlic powder plus 2 to 2 1/2 teaspoon water

FERMENTED SOYBEAN PASTE/TAO JIAO (South Asian flavoring agent) – 1 tablespoon See also MISO
- ☞ 1 1/2 teaspoons Japanese dark miso, such as *hatcho*, or Korean soybean paste/*doenjang*
- ☞ 2 teaspoons Chinese black bean sauce/*douchi jiang*

FERMENTED SOYBEAN SAUCE/SALTED SOYBEANS/TAUCHEO/TAUCO/TAUEO (Indonesian and Malaysian seasoning) – 1 tablespoon
- ☞ 1 tablespoon Thai soybean paste/fermented soybeans/*tao jiao*

FERMENTED TOASTED SOYBEAN DISK/TUA NAO KHAAP (South Asian seasoning) – 1 tablespoon chopped or crumbled disk
- ☞ 1 tablespoon toasted chickpea flour plus 1 teaspoon Japanese brown miso paste
- ☞ 2 tablespoons Thai soybean paste/fermented soybean/*dao jiao*

FIDDLEHEAD FERNS/OSTRICH FERNS/KOSARI/WARABI/ZENMAI
(young, unfurled ostrich sprouts) – 1 pound fresh or frozen
- ☞ 1 pound pencil-thin fresh asparagus or haricots verts, blanched in boiling water until crisp-tender, then refreshed in ice water

FILIPINO SPICY CURED SAUSAGE See CHORIZO DE BILBAO

FINGERROOT/CHINESE KEYS/CHINESE GINGER/KRACHAI, FRESH
(Southeast Asian seasoning) – 1-inch piece (1 tablespoon peeled and finely chopped)
- ☞ 2 teaspoons brined fingerroot slivers, well drained and rinsed
- ☞ 1 1/2 tablespoons jarred galanga/Ka Chai (rinse to remove brine, then finely chop)
- ☞ 1 tablespoon finely chopped fresh or frozen greater galangal
- ☞ 1 1/2 teaspoons kencur powder (ground Kaempferia galanga)
- ☞ 2 scant teaspoons finely chopped fresh young ginger

FISH FLAKES, DRIED/KATSUOBUSHI (Japanese dried bonito/skipjack tuna flakes) – 1 loosely packed cup See also DASHI
- ☞ 1 cup dried mackerel flakes/sababushi (for soups and stocks; less expensive)
- ☞ 1 cup bonito thread shavings/ito-kezuri katsuo (for garnish on salads and tofu)
- ☞ 1 cup dried baby sardines or anchovies/iniko/niboshi, dry-roasted until very crisp, 20 minutes, then cooled and ground (stronger tasting; use according to taste)
- ☞ 1 cup ready-to-use dried baby anchovies or tiny whitebait/ikan teri/ikan bilis/jiang yu zi, rinsed and lightly pounded (stronger; use according to taste)
- ☞ 1 ikan bilis stock cube, or part thereof (for soups and stocks)

FISH MINT/FISH SCALE MINT/RAU DIEP CA/VAP CA (Vietnamese seasoning) – 1 ounce
- ☞ 1 ounce fresh spearmint, young sorrel, lemon basil, or Thai basil

☞ 1 ounce unsprayed variegated chameleon plant/*Houttuynia cordata* (use the top leaves)

FISH PASTE, FERMENTED *See ASIAN FISH PASTE*

FISH SAUCE/NAM PLA/NUOC NAM/PATIS/SHOTTSURU/TUK TREY
(Southeast Asian salty liquid seasoning) – 1 tablespoon
☞ 1 tablespoon Vietnamese vegetarian fish sauce/*nuoc mam an chay*
☞ 1 tablespoon Japanese *ayu* sweet fish sauce (more delicate) or *ishiri* fermented squid sauce (stronger flavor)
☞ 2 to 3 teaspoons Thai unfiltered fish sauce/*pla ra* or *pla ra* powder (stronger flavor)
☞ 1 tablespoon Vietnamese anchovy sauce/*mam nem* or Italian anchovy sauce/syrup/*colatura di alici*
☞ 2 teaspoons anchovy paste mixed with 1/2 teaspoon soy sauce or Maggi Seasoning
☞ 1 1/2 teaspoons each Golden Mountain Seasoning sauce and soy sauce
☞ 1 tablespoon soy sauce and 1 finely minced anchovy fillet
☞ 2 tablespoons white or Thai soy sauce
☞ 1/4 teaspoon salt (or to taste)

FISH SAUCE, VEGETARIAN – 1/4 cup
☞ 1/4 cup coconut aminos plus 1 teaspoon sea salt
Make Your Own Break 1 small dried shiitake mushroom into pieces and combine with 1/2 cup water plus 1 1/2 teaspoons each sea salt and soy sauce. Simmer until reduced by half. Strain, cool, and store in the refrigerator. It will keep for up to 3 weeks.

FISH STOCK *See STOCK, FISH*

FISH, FATTY (more than 6% of fat by weight) – 1 pound:
☞ 1 pound bonito, black cod/sablefish/sable, herring, mackerel, pilchard, pompano, salmon, sardine, shad, smelt, sturgeon, trout (rainbow and lake), yellowtail, and whitebait

FISH, LEAN (less than 2% fat by weight; some belong to the same, or related species, but identified or known by different names) – 1 pound

➢ 1 pound branzino/Mediterranean sea bass, barramundi, bass (white sea and black sea), Cape capensis, brill, catfish, char, cod (scrod), croaker/drum, cusk, flatfish, flounder, fluke, grouper, haddock, hake, halibut (Atlantic, California, Pacific), John Dory, moi, monkfish tail, orange roughy, perch, pike, pickerel, plaice, pollock/coley, porgy/sea bream/dorade, redfish/red drum, red snapper, rockfish, sand dab, sculpin, sea bass, shark, skate, sole (Dover, lemon, petrale, Rex), tautog/blackfish, tilapia, tilefish, turbot, walleye, or whiting

FISH, MODERATELY FATTY (between 2% and 6% fat by weight) – 1 pound

➢ 1 pound barracuda, bluefish, carp, mahi-mahi/dolphinfish, mullet, striped bass, swordfish, tuna, yellowtail, and whitefish

FISH, WHOLE – 8 ounces to 3 pounds

➢ Arctic char, barramundi, branzino/European bass, black bass, butterfish/pomfret, carp, small catfish, dorade/sea bream, flounder, gray mullet (striped and silver), grouper, herring, lake perch, mackerel, plaice, pompano/yellowtail, rainbow trout, rockfish, sea bass, scrod, snapper, striped bass, golden or black tilapia

FIVE-SPICE MIX, INDIAN *See BENGALI FIVE-SPICE MIX*

FIVE-SPICE POWDER, CHINESE *See CHINESE FIVE-SPICE POWDER*

FLOUR, ATTA/PATENT DURA *See ATTA/PATENT DURA FLOUR*

FLOUR, BESAN *See BESAN/GRAM FLOUR*

FLOUR, BROWN RICE *See RICE FLOUR, BROWN*

FLOUR, GRAM *See BESAN/GRAM FLOUR*

FLOUR, JAPANESE RICE/JOSHINKO See RICE FLOUR, WHITE SUPERFINE

FLOUR, JAPANESE SOFT/HAKURIK-KO See JAPANESE SOFT FLOUR

FLOUR, LOTUS ROOT/ŎU FEN See LOTUS ROOT FLOUR

FLOUR, MAIDA See MAIDA

FLOUR, MUNG BEAN See MUNG BEAN FLOUR/STARCH/POWDER

FLOUR, SINGODA See SINGODA FLOUR

FLOUR, SOBA/KISOBA See JAPANESE SOBA FLOUR

FLOUR, SOOJI See SOOJI/SUJI/RAWA

FLOUR, ROASTED BARLEY/TSAMPA See TSAMPA

FLOUR, ROASTED SOYBEAN FLOUR/KINOKO See KINOKO

FLOUR, SWEET/GLUTINOUS RICE See RICE FLOUR, SWEET/GLUTINOUS

FLOUR, TAPIOCA See TAPIOCA STARCH/FLOUR

FLOUR, TEMPURA See TEMPURA FLOUR

FLOUR, URAD DAL See URAD DAL FLOUR

FLOUR, WATER CHESTNUT See WATER CHESTNUT STARCH/POWDER

FLOUR, WHITE RICE, SUPERFINE OR ASIAN See RICE FLOUR, WHITE SUPERFINE

FLOWERING QUINCE (Chinese or Japanese firm, sour fruit) – 1 pound
 ➫ 1 pound green Mexican papaya

FLOWERS/BLOSSOMS/PETALS, FRESH EDIBLE – 1 cup for salads and garnish

- ☞ 1 cup non-sprayed, pesticide-free anise hyssop, apple, arugula, basil (including African blue basil), bachelor's buttons/cornflower, bee balm, begonia, bergamot, bok choy, borage, broccoli, cabbage, calendula, chervil, chickweed, chicory, flowering chive, miner's lettuce/claytonia, clover, collards, crowder peas, daisy, dandelion, daylily, dill, elderflower, fava, fennel, French marigold, geranium, hibiscus, hollyhock, kale, lavender, leek, lemon, lovage, pot marigold, marjoram, Mexican tarragon/Mexican mint marigold, mustard greens, nasturtium, onion, orange, oregano, pansy, parsley, peach, peas, perilla, pineapple, plum, primrose, radish, sage, stock, squash, thyme, turnip, viola, violet, or sweet woodruff
- ☞ 1 cup rose petals (rugosa and pink damask especially; cut off the white part at the base of each petal, as it is bitter)

FOOD WRAPPERS See WRAPPERS FOR FOOD, NON-EDIBLE; WRAPPERS FOR FOOD, VEGETABLE-BASED

FURIKAKE (Japanese sesame and seaweed condiment for rice) – 1 tablespoon

- ☞ 1 tablespoon dried nori shreds with sesame seed/nori komi furikake
- ☞ 1 tablespoon flaked or shredded green nori/ao-nori
- ☞ 1 tablespoon toasted black sesame seeds/kura goma
- ☞ 1 tablespoon powdered purple shiso leaves and sea salt/yukari/shiso yukari/shiso furikake
- ☞ 1 tablespoon toasted sesame seed and sea salt/gomashio;
- ☞ 1 tablespoon dried nori, alaria/winged kelp, or dulse, toasted then crushed by hand

FUSHIMI PEPPER, FRESH/FUSHIMI-TOGARASHI (Japanese mild chili pepper) – 1 or 2

- ☞ 2 or 3 Spanish padrón peppers
- ☞ 3 or 4 Japanese shishito peppers
- ☞ 1 Anaheim chili or Cubanelle pepper, cut into strips

G

GAI LAN See CHINESE BROCCOLI

GALANGAL, GREATER/LAOS/LENGKUAS (Southeast Asian seasoning root) – 1 1/2-inch slice fresh or frozen (1 tablespoon peeled and finely chopped)
- 4 teaspoons chopped pickled galangal/*kha*
- 3 or more (1/8-inch) slices dried galangal root/galanga soaked in hot water 30 minutes, then squeezed dry
- 1 tablespoon galangal paste
- 1 1/2 teaspoons (or more) Indonesian Laos powder (dried ground galangal root; less flavorful)
- 1-inch piece fresh young ginger (or 2 or 3 teaspoons finely chopped) plus a few grains of ground black pepper, or a few drops of lemon juice, or a small pinch of finely chopped lemongrass

GALANGAL, LESSER/KAEMPFERIA/KENKUR/AROMATIC GINGER – 1 1/2-inch slice fresh or frozen (1 tablespoon peeled and finely chopped)
- 3 or more (1/8-inch) slices dried sand ginger soaked in hot water 30 minutes, then squeezed dry
- 2 teaspoons sand ginger powder/zedoary root powder
- 1 1/2 to 2 tablespoons peeled and finely chopped fresh ginger root (less pungent)

GARAM MASALA (Indian all-purpose aromatic seasoning) – 1 tablespoon
- 1 teaspoon mild/sweet curry powder
- 1/2 teaspoon each ground toasted coriander and cumin

GARLIC CHIVES/CHINESE LEEKS/NIRA GRASS/JUMYIT – 1 ounce (1/4 cup finely chopped)
- 1 or 2 sliced garlic leaves (cut the leaves when plants are no more than 8 inches tall)
- 1/4 cup snipped Western chives or thinly sliced scallion or green onion greens plus 1 scant teaspoon minced garlic

GARLIC OIL (Asian condiment) – 1/4 cup
Make Your Own Crush 2 large garlic cloves and cook in 1/4 cup peanut oil over low heat, stirring occasionally, until light brown, 4 to 5 minutes. (Do not let the garlic become too dark or it will be bitter.) Cool and strain, discarding the garlic. Use immediately, or refrigerate in a small sterilized jar for up to 1 week.

GARLIC PASTE/PUREE, ROASTED – 1/4 cup
Make Your Own Toast unpeeled garlic cloves from 2 large garlic heads in a dry skillet over medium heat for 7 or 8 minutes, then squeeze through a garlic press (remove the peels in the press as needed). Or roast the unpeeled garlic, tightly wrapped in foil, in a preheated 425°F oven for 35 to 45 minutes (slice 1/2 inch from the top of the garlic heads and drizzle with 1 teaspoon olive oil before roasting).

GARLIC SHOOTS, YOUNG GREEN/GARLIC SCAPES – 1 cup
- 1 cup thinly sliced young scallions, green garlic/young garlic, or garlic chives
- 2/3 cup finely chopped chives plus scant 1/3 cup finely chopped garlic
- 1/2 cup chopped garlic

GARLIC, BLACK FERMENTED See FERMENTED BLACK GARLIC

GARLIC, FRESH – 1 medium clove (1 teaspoon minced or pressed)
- 1 thawed frozen garlic cube, such as Dorot, crushed
- 1 tablespoon green fresh garlic/wet garlic (milder and juicier)
- 1 tablespoon finely minced garlic chives

☞ 1/2 teaspoon garlic juice, garlic flakes, or instant garlic

☞ 1 teaspoon garlic paste from a tube, or jarred minced garlic

☞ 1/4 teaspoon granulated garlic, or dried minced garlic softened in 1 teaspoon water, about 10 minutes

☞ 1/8 teaspoon garlic powder

☞ 1/2 teaspoon garlic salt; reduce the salt in the recipe by 1/2 teaspoon

☞ 1 small shallot or 1 medium shallot lobe, finely minced (1 tablespoon)

☞ 1/2 medium clove (or 1/2 teaspoon minced) wild/meadow garlic or field/crow garlic

☞ 1 to 2 teaspoons garlic vinegar (if compatible)

GARLIC, GREEN/YOUNG GARLIC – 2 stalks minced (white and tender green parts only)

☞ 2 stalks garlic chives, garlic scapes (curly garlic shoots), or Chinese garlic stems

☞ 3 scallions (white and tender green parts only)

☞ 2 garlic cloves blanched in boiling water 1 minute, then minced

GARLIC, PICKLED *See CHINESE PICKLED GARLIC*

GHEE/USLI GHEE (Indian-style clarified butter with a higher smoke point than regular clarified butter) – 1 tablespoon

☞ 1 tablespoon vegetable ghee/*vanaspati*

☞ 1 tablespoon refined or virgin coconut oil

☞ 1 tablespoon extra-virgin macadamia oil

☞ 1 tablespoon clarified butter (lower smoke point)

☞ 2 teaspoons unsalted butter plus 1 teaspoon corn or sunflower oil (lower smoke point)

GINGELLY OIL/GINGILI OIL/TIL OIL (Indian and Burmese cooking oil) – 1 cup

☞ 3/4 cup untoasted sesame oil and 1/4 cup toasted sesame oil

☞ 2/3 cup vegetable oil and 1/3 cup toasted sesame oil

GINGER-GARLIC PASTE/ADRAK LEHSUN KA PASTE (Indian seasoning) – 1/2 (scant) cup

Make Your Own Process 1/3 cup coarsely chopped fresh ginger, 1/3 cup coarsely chopped fresh garlic, and 1 tablespoon water in a blender or food processor until reduced to a fine paste. Store in a sterilized jar in the refrigerator; it will keep for up to 1 month.

GINGER JUICE – 1 tablespoon (or more)

Make Your Own Peel a 1 1/2- to 2-inch piece of fresh ginger (about 1 1/2 to 2 ounces), finely grate it, and then press through a garlic press, tea strainer, fine-mesh sieve, or cheesecloth. (Freezing and thawing the ginger will produce more juice.)

GINGER JUICE – 6 tablespoons to 1 scant cup

Make Your Own Wash 1 pound unpeeled fresh ginger then chop or thinly slice (it should yield 2 1/2 to 3 cups). Process in a blender or food processor for 3 to 5 minutes, then strain in a cheesecloth-lined sieve, pressing on solids to extract all the liquid. It will keep in the refrigerator for up to 1 week, or freeze for longer storage.

GINGER PASTE/PISSA ADRAK/AADA BATA (Indian seasoning) – 1/3 cup

⮞ 4 ounces scrubbed fresh ginger grated on a rasp-type grater

Make Your Own Process 1/2 cup peeled chopped ginger and a pinch of salt in a food processor until reduced to a paste, adding a little water if necessary. (Cut the ginger lengthwise first, then against the grain.)

GINGER SOY SAUCE – 1 cup

⮞ 1 cup light soy sauce and 1 tablespoon ginger juice

GINGER SYRUP – 1 cup

⮞ 1 cup syrup from jarred preserved stem ginger (for 1 tablespoon, mix 1 teaspoon honey with 1 tablespoon ginger juice)

Make Your Own Bring to a boil 1/3 cup thinly sliced peeled ginger, 1/2 cup firmly packed brown sugar, and 1 cup water, then simmer until reduced and syrupy, about 10 minutes. Cool then strain; store, refrigerated, for up to 1 month. (For more intense flavor, let the syrup sit for 45 to 60 minutes before straining.)

Or

Add 2/3 cup peeled and sliced fresh ginger to 1 cup heated heavy syrup; cool while covered, then steep for 2 days before straining. Store, refrigerated, for up to 1 month.

GINGER VINEGAR – 1 cup

Make Your Own Bring 1 cup cider vinegar, 1/4 cup peeled sliced fresh ginger, and 2 teaspoons sugar to a boil. Cool while covered, then steep in a cool, dark place for 10 days before straining. It will keep, refrigerated, for up to 3 months.

GINGER, PICKLED/GARI/AMAZU SHOGA/BENI SHOGA (Japanese sushi accompaniment) – 1 cup

Make Your Own Bring to a boil 1 cup peeled and very thinly sliced fresh ginger (about 4 ounces), 1/2 cup unseasoned rice vinegar, and 1/4 cup granulated sugar (or less if desired); cool, then transfer to a jar. Cover, and refrigerate for 3 or 4 days before using. It will keep in the refrigerator for up to 12 months. (For *beni shoga*, shred rather than slice the ginger and add a little beet juice or a drop of food coloring; for *amazu shoga* use the young tender ginger shoot, which turns pink automatically.)

GINGER, POWDERED See GINGER, DRIED GROUND/POWDERED

GINGER, STEM, PRESERVED IN SYRUP – 2 tablespoons
- ⮕ 2 teaspoons thinly sliced soft/uncrystallized ginger; or crystallized ginger, rinsed (for ginger)
- ⮕ 2 tablespoons ginger syrup (for syrup)

GINGER, YOUNG FRESH – 2 ounces sliced
- ⮕ 2 ounces mature ginger, peeled, sliced, and rinsed in salted water to reduce its pungency

GINKGO NUTS/GINNAN/EUNHAENG, FRESH (Japanese and Korean) – 1 dozen shelled and blanched for cooking
- 1 (3.5-ounce) package gingko nuts, shelled and peeled
- 1 dozen canned ginkgo nuts, rinsed
- 1 dozen fresh wild ginkgo nuts/*Ginkgo biloba*, baked for 1 hour at 300°F, then shelled and any remaining skin rubbed off
- 1/4 cup shelled green peas (lacks bitterness)

GINSENG ROOT, AGED/PANAX (Chinese seasoning agent) – 1 ounce (2 tablespoons minced)
- 1 ounce fine side roots, stem bits, shavings, or sun-dried white ginseng (less expensive)
- 1 ounce dried precut bellflower root/vine/codonopsis/*doraji/dang shen* (for soups and other cooked dishes; not as strong but less expensive; soak root overnight then squeeze dry)
- 2 ginseng-root tea bags (for fresh minced or dried ground ginseng)

GOJI BERRY/WOLFBERRY/GOUQI /GAU GEI JEE/JI ZI//KUKO, DRIED (Chinese flavoring) – 1 cup
- 1 cup dried jujubes (Chinese red dates)
- 1 cup dried Chilean wineberries/maqui berries
- 1 cup dried cranberries, barberries, or mulberries
- 2 to 3 tablespoons goji berry powder (for drinks and smoothies)

GOLDEN MOUNTAIN SAUCE/TUONG QIA VI (Thai seasoning sauce) – 1 tablespoon
- 1 tablespoon Maggi Seasoning or Healthy Boy Stir Fry Seasoning Sauce,

GOLDEN NEEDLES See LILY BUDS

GOMASHIO/GOMASIO See SESAME SALT

GOOSE FAT, RENDERED – 1 tablespoon
- 1 tablespoon rendered duck fat, pork fat, tallow, or leaf lard

☞ 1 tablespoon fruity olive oil, or 1 1/2 teaspoons each oil and unsalted butter

GORAKA/GAMBODGE (Sri Lankan souring agent) – 4 dried segments ground to a pulp (1 tablespoon)
☞ 1 tablespoon tamarind concentrate
☞ 1 tablespoon bitter orange juice, lemon juice, or lime juice

GOSARI See FIDDLEHEAD FERNS

GOTU KOLA/GOTUKOLLE/BUA BOK/PENNYWORT, ASIATIC – 1 bunch (4 ounces/1 cup sprigs)
☞ 1 cup baby arugula leaves, flat-leaf (Italian) parsley, or watercress sprigs

GOURD (angle/luffa, bottle, turban, wax/winter gourd) See SQUASH, ASIAN

GOURD STRIPS, DRIED/KAMPYO (Japanese long, thin food wrappers) – 1 dozen
☞ 1 dozen fresh chives, dipped into boiling water for 1 or 2 seconds, rinsed in cold water, then patted dry
☞ 12 long strips of cucumber peel, sliced lengthwise into thin ribbons, dipped into boiling water until softened, then patted dry

GRAIN SYRUP See KOREAN GRAIN SYRUP

GRAM FLOUR See BESAN

GREEN MANGO See MANGO, GREEN

GREENS, ASIAN BLEND – 1 pound
☞ 1 pound Chinese spinach/amaranth, Chinese mustard greens, garland chrysanthemum, mizuna, and/or tatsoi

GUNPOWDER TEA (Chinese pelleted, slightly smoky, green tea) – 1 cup brewed
- ⊳ 1 cup fine-quality Japanese or Chinese green tea

GYOZA WRAPPERS/JIAOZI (Japanese pot sticker wrappers) – 1 pound
- ⊳ 1 pound round wonton wrappers, preferably Chinese which are thicker, or square wrappers with the corners cut off (thinner and smaller)
- ⊳ 1 pound empanada wrappers
- ⊳ 1 pound dumpling skins/*siu mai/suey gow/shao mai* (thinner)
- ⊳ 1 pound egg roll wrappers, cut into circles using a 3-inch cutter (thicker)

H

HAJIKAMI (Japanese sweet pickled young ginger) See GINGER, PICKLED

HALLABONG JUICE (Korean citrus fruit) – 1 tablespoon
- ⊯ 1 1/2 teaspoons each orange and tangerine juice

HATCHO MISO (Japanese dark brown, soybean-based miso) – 1 tablespoon
- ⊯ 1 tablespoon red miso/*inaka miso/sendai miso*
- ⊯ 1 tablespoon *akadashi miso* (*hatcho* and *saikyo* miso blend)

HATO MUGI/COIX LACRYMA-JOBI (Japanese whole-grain barley) – 1 pound
- ⊯ 1 pound pearl barley (smaller grain; slightly different flavor)

HIJIKI/HIZIKI (Japanese sun-dried black strand seaweed) – 1 ounce
- ⊯ 1 ounce refrigerated *mozuku* (lighter flavor; stringy shreds; soak for 10 minutes or add directly to soup)
- ⊯ 1 ounce arame (milder and less salty, longer thinner strands; soak for 5 minutes; less cooking time)
- ⊯ 1 ounce kiri kombu (stronger flavor; long narrow strips; soak for 10 minutes)
- ⊯ 1 ounce wakame (soak for 10 to 20 minutes; cut out the tough center rib, then slice the rest into thin ribbons)

HING See ASAFETIDA

HOG PLUM/MAKAWK (Southeast Asian souring agent) – 1 pound peeled
- ⊯ 12 ounces tomatillos, green or unripe cherry tomatoes, or gooseberries

HOISIN SAUCE/HÓI SÌN JÌANG (Chinese thick, sweet cooking condiment) – 1/4 cup
- 1/4 cup Chee hou sauce plus 1 or 2 teaspoons brown sugar or dark-bodied honey
- 2 tablespoons each oyster sauce and thick tomato sauce

Make Your Own Whisk together 2 tablespoons thick barbecue sauce, 1 tablespoon each molasses and dark soy sauce, and 1/2 teaspoon Chinese five-spice powder.

HOKKAIDO/POTIMARON/RED KURI (Japanese squash) – 1 pound
- 1 pound Baby Red Hubbard, Fairytale, Sugar, or pie pumpkin (for Orange Hokkaido)
- 1 pound buttercup, butternut, Carnival, or acorn squash (for Green Hokkaido)

HONEY, LYCHEE See LYCHEE HONEY

HORSERADISH LEAVES/MALUNGGAY DAHOON (Indian and Filipino vegetable) – 8 ounces
- 8 ounces baby spinach, mizuna, or tatsoi

I

IDIAPPAM/IDIAPA, DRIED (South Indian and Sri Lankan thin rice noodles) – 1 pound
- 1 pound dried Thai rice sticks/*sen yai/phat*, Chinese rice vermicelli/ *mi fen/mai fun*, Vietnamese rice noodles/*banh pho kho*, or Filipino rice stick noodles/*pancit bihon*

IKURA (Japanese salmon roe) – 1 ounce
- 1 ounce capelin/*masago*, carp or red mullet/*tarama*, codfish/*tarako*, flying fish/*tobiko*, scallop, smelt/*ebikko*, steelhead, or French trout roe
- 1 ounce whitefish/American Golden Caviar roe (yellow-gold), sea urchin/*uni* (rich gold to light yellow), or herring roe/*kazunoko* (pink/ yellow)
- 1 ounce salted Alaskan pollock roe/*momojiko* (red) or flavored with chili powder/*mentaiko* (deep red)
- 1 ounce red vegetarian caviar (such as Cavi-art derived from seaweed)

INDIAN COOKING CREAM *See MALAI*

INDIAN LEEK ROOT *See GARLIC CHIVES*

INDONESIAN FISH SAUCE/KECAP IKAN/KETJAP IKAN *See FISH SAUCE*

INDONESIAN SOY SAUCE *See KECAP ASIN; KECAP MANIS*

INDONESIAN VINEGAR/CUKA – 1 tablespoon
- 1 tablespoon distilled colorless malt vinegar or rice vinegar

J

JACKFRUIT/JAKFRUIT/KATHAL, FRESH OR FROZEN (Indian and Southeast Asian fruit and vegetable) – 1-pound section
- 2 (20-ounce) cans jackfruit in brine, drained and rinsed (for mature, yellow fruit) or drained young (green) jackfruit in brine (for young green fruit)
- 1 large Hawaiian papaya, or 1-pound piece of peeled and seeded Mexican papaya (for mature, yellow fruit)
- 1 (1-pound section) winter melon or breadfruit, 2 medium chayote squash, 1 or 2 unripe plantains, or 3 medium boiling potatoes (for young green fruit)

JAGGERY/PALM SUGAR/GUR (Southeast Asian dark, unrefined sugar) – 1 cup grated, shaved, granulated, or jarred
- 1 cup jaggery powder
- 1 cup grated or crushed Mexican unrefined sugar/*piloncillo/panela* or *panocha/panucha*
- 1 cup crushed/grated Indonesian palm sugar/*gula jawa* or Malaysian palm sugar/*gula melaka*
- 1 cup dark Muscovado/Barbados sugar
- 1 cup dark brown unrefined cane sugar, such as Natural Molasses
- 3/4 cup granulated sugar plus 5 tablespoons molasses
- 1 cup dark brown or maple sugar moistened to a coarse paste with 1 tablespoon light molasses (or jarred palm sugar)

JAGGERY POWDER (Southeast Asian sweetener) – 1 ounce
- 1 cup grated, shaved, granulated, or jarred jaggery

JAPANESE BLACK SUGAR/KUROZATO/KURO SATO (dark unrefined sugar) – 1 cup chopped
- 1 cup chopped or shaved Mexican unrefined sugar/*piloncillo/panela*

- ☞ 1 cup Indian palm sugar/jaggery/*gur* or Indonesian palm sugar/*gula jawa*
- ☞ 1 cup firmly packed dark brown sugar plus 1 tablespoon unsulphured molasses
- ☞ 1 cup dark brown molasses unrefined cane sugar, such as Billington's

JAPANESE BLACK SUGAR SYRUP/KUROMITSU – 1 cup
- ☞ 1 cup dark corn syrup or blackstrap molasses

JAPANESE BLACK VINEGAR/AGED RICE VINEGAR/KUROZU – 1 tablespoon
- ☞ 1 tablespoon balsamic vinegar or good-quality sherry vinegar

JAPANESE BROWN RICE VINEGAR/GENMAIZU – 1 tablespoon
- ☞ 2 teaspoons cider or balsamic vinegar and 1 teaspoon water
- ☞ 1 tablespoon unseasoned rice wine vinegar

JAPANESE CHILI OIL/RAYU – 1 teaspoon
- ☞ 1 teaspoon toasted sesame oil and 1/2 teaspoon Japanese spice mixture *shichimi togarashi*
- ☞ Chinese chili oil

JAPANESE CHILI POWDER/ICHIMI TOGARASHI – 1 teaspoon
- ☞ 3/4 teaspoon Chinese ground red pepper
- ☞ 1/2 teaspoon Hungarian or mild Spanish paprika, or ground cayenne pepper

JAPANESE CHIVES/BUNCHING ONION/ASATSUKI – 1 tablespoon
- ☞ 1 tablespoon finely snipped green part of scallions or green onions
- ☞ 1 tablespoon finely snipped sprouted tips of yellow or white onion

JAPANESE CITRUS FRUIT *See KABOSU; SUDACHI; YUZU*

JAPANESE CUCUMBER/KYURI – 1
- ☞ 1 Lebanese/Persian cucumber

☞ 2 tender-skinned Kirby or pickling cucumbers
☞ 1/2 English/hothouse cucumber

JAPANESE CURRY POWDER – 1 tablespoon
☞ 1 tablespoon mild, sweet-flavored curry powder, such as S&B Oriental Curry Powder
☞ 1 tablespoon mild Madras curry powder (spicier)

JAPANESE DAIKON & RED PEPPER CONDIMENT/GARNISH/MOMIJI OROSHI – 1/4 cup
☞ 1/2 teaspoon red chili yuzu paste/*yuzu koshu* mixed with 1/4 cup grated drained daikon (adds citrus flavor)
☞ 1/4 cup grated daikon tip/*daikon oroshi* (lacks heat)

JAPANESE DIPPING SAUCE *See ASIAN DIPPING SAUCE; PONZU SAUCE; TEMPURA DIPPING SAUCE*

JAPANESE EGGPLANT/NASU – 1 (about 6 ounces)
☞ 1 slender Asian/Indian or Persian eggplant
☞ 3 or 4 Thai green eggplants (not pea/baby eggplants)
☞ 1/4 globe eggplant, peeled and cut into strips

JAPANESE FERN SHOOTS/WARABI – 1 pound
☞ 1 pound baby asparagus or skinny asparagus spears
☞ 1 pound Chinese yard-long beans

JAPANESE FERMENTED CHILI PASTE *See KANZURI*

JAPANESE FIELD POTATOES/SATOIMO – 1 pound (about 8)
☞ 1 pound small taro roots/dasheen (best when served immediately upon cooking)
☞ 1 pound small baby white potatoes (use small sweet potatoes for Japanese pale-fleshed sweet potatoes/*satsuma-imo*)

JAPANESE FISH SAUCE/SHOTTSURU/ISHIRI/ISHIRU – *1 teaspoon*
- ⊨ 1 teaspoon Japanese fermented sweet fish sauce/*ayu* (more mellow)
- ⊨ 1 teaspoon Thai fish sauce/*nam pla*, Vietnamese fish sauce/*nuoc nam*, Filipino fish sauce/ *patis*, or any Asian fermented fish sauce
- ⊨ 1 to 2 teaspoons anchovy paste or finely chopped anchovies

JAPANESE GOMA PASTE *See SESAME PASTE*

JAPANESE GREEN ONION/LONG ONION/WELSH ONION/TOKYO NEGI/ NAGA NEGI – *1 regular stalk*
- ⊨ 2 or 3 Mexican onions or large thick scallions

JAPANESE GREEN PEPPER/AO TOGARASHI *See SHISHITO PEPPER*

JAPANESE HORSERADISH *See WASABI; WASABI, POWDERED; WASABI, PREPARED*

JAPANESE HOT RED CHILI/SANTAKA/TOGARASHI JAPONES/TAKANOT-SUME, FRESH OR DRIED – *1*
- ⊨ 1 fresh cayenne, japonés, serrano, or Thai chili
- ⊨ 1 dried de árbol, cayenne, serrano, or Thai chili
- ⊨ 1 teaspoon ground Japanese chili/*ichimi togarashi*
- ⊨ 1 teaspoon ground cayenne pepper; or crushed red pepper flakes
- ⊨ 1 1/4 teaspoons seven-spice seasoning/*shichimi togarashi*

JAPANESE KOBE BEEF – *1 pound*
- ⊨ 1 pound American Wagyu or Washugyu (Kobe-style beef; a cross between Japanese Black Wagyu and American Black Angus)
- ⊨ 1 pound American prime beef
- ⊨ 1 pound Italian Chianina or French Charolais beef

JAPANESE KUROBUTA PORK – *1 pound*
- ⊨ 1 pound American Berkshire, Berkshire-Duroc blend, Duroc, or Red Wattle pork

JAPANESE MAYONNAISE/TOMAGO-NO-MOTO – 1/4 cup
☞ 1 tablespoon Kewpie brand or any light, creamy mayonnaise
☞ 1 tablespoon Western-style mayonnaise, 1/2 teaspoon rice vinegar, and 1/8 teaspoon superfine sugar, stirred until the sugar dissolves

JAPANESE MOUNTAIN YAMS/YAMAIMO – 1 pound
☞ 1 pound red skinned yams, such as Garnet or Jewel (less gelatinous)

JAPANESE MUSTARD/KARASHI See MUSTARD, JAPANESE

JAPANESE MUSTARD SPINACH See KOMATSUA

JAPANESE NIHAIZU SAUCE BASE See NIHAIZU

JAPANESE NOODLES, BEAN THREAD/BEAN VERMICELLI/HARUSAME/ SAIFUN – 8 ounces
☞ 8 ounces Chinese mung bean thread noodles/*fen si,* Korean sweet potato vermicelli/*dang myun,* Thai cellophane noodles/*woon sen,* or Vietnamese cellophane noodles/*bun tau*
☞ 8 ounces *itokonnyaku* noodles, rinsed and drained (brownish colored; thicker; more gelatinous)
☞ 8 ounces *shirataki* noodles, rinsed and drained (white colored; thinner; more gelatinous)
☞ 8 ounces agar-agar noodles/*yang fen,* rinsed and drained (transparent; thinner; more gelatinous)

JAPANESE NOODLES, BUCKWHEAT/SOBA/CHA SOBA, FRESH OR DRIED – 1 pound
☞ 1 pound fresh or dried 100% buckwheat flour noodles/*juwari soba,*
☞ 1 pound fresh or dried 80% buckwheat flour and 20% wheat flour noodles/*nippachi soba* (milder)
☞ 1 pound fresh or dried whole-grain buckwheat noodles/*hikigurumi soba* (darker, with a rougher texture)
☞ 1 pound fresh or dried Korean buckwheat noodles/*naeng myun*
☞ 1 pound fresh or dried buckwheat and mountain yam soba noodles/ *yamaimo soba* (paler and chewier)

☞ 1 pound dried Kamut or spelt soba noodles, such as Eden Organic

☞ 1 pound dried whole-wheat or brown rice vermicelli (add salt to the cooking water)

JAPANESE NOODLES, THICK WHEAT/UDON, FRESH OR FROZEN – 18 ounces (2 packages)

☞ 14 ounces dried udon noodles, *sanuki* udon noodles (thicker and chewier), or *inaniwa* udon noodles (thinner; more delicate)

☞ 18 ounces fresh or 14 ounces dried *kishimen/himokawa* noodles (thicker and wider)

☞ 14 ounces dried linguine noodles

JAPANESE NOODLES, THIN WHEAT/SOMEN/TAMAGO SOMEN, DRIED – 14 ounces

☞ 14 ounces dried *hiyamugi* noodles, Filipino *miswa* noodles, or Indian *misoa* noodles

☞ 14 ounces dried angel hair, spaghettini, or vermicelli pasta

JAPANESE NOODLES, THIN WHEAT EGG/RAMEN, FRESH – 1 pound

☞ 1 pound Chinese wo mein, lo mein, or chow mein noodles

☞ 1 pound spaghettini or vermicelli pasta

JAPANESE OKINAWA POTATOES (purple sweet potatoes) – 1 pound

☞ 1 pound Hawaiian Molokai sweet potatoes, or other purple sweet potatoes, such as Stokes

JAPANESE OKONOMIYAKI SAUCE See OKONOMIYAKI SAUCE

JAPANESE PEARL BARLEY See HATO MUGI

JAPANESE PICKLED CABBAGE/QUICK PICKLES/TSUKEMONO/SHIO ZUKE – 3 cups

Make Your Own Toss 4 cups coarsely shredded napa cabbage with 2 teaspoons coarse salt in a freezer bag; press out the air, seal, and refrigerate for 2 to 3 days, turning the bag daily. Drain, rinse with water, then squeeze out the water. Use within 2 to 3 days. For instant pickling, rub the cabbage vigorously with salt until tender and reduced to half, about 10 minutes, then squeeze out excess water.

JAPANESE PLUM, SALT-PICKLED See UMEBOSHI; UMEBOSHI PASTE

JAPANESE PLUM WINE See PLUM WINE

JAPANESE PONZU SAUCE See PONZU SAUCE

JAPANESE POTATO See JAPANESE FIELD POTATOES; JAPANESE MOUNTAIN YAMS; JAPANESE OKINAWA POTATOES; JAPANESE PRAWN POTATOES

JAPANESE PRAWN POTATOES/EBI-IMO – 1 pound
 ↣ 1 pound Japanese field potatoes/sato-imo (coarser texture)

JAPANESE PURPLE SWEET POTATO VINEGAR/BENIMOSU – 1 tablespoon
 ↣ 1 tablespoon sherry vinegar or balsamic vinegar

JAPANESE RADISH See DAIKON

JAPANESE RAPE BLOSSOMS/FLOWERING TOPS/NANOHANA – 1 pound
 ↣ 1 pound thin broccoli raab/rapini

JAPANESE RICE – See RICE, JAPANESE SHORT-GRAIN JAPONICA; RICE, JAPANESE, SWEET/GLUTINOUS

JAPANESE RICE FLOUR/JOSHINKO – See RICE FLOUR, WHITE SUPERFINE

JAPANESE RICE VINEGAR, PURE/JUNMAI ZU/GENMAI MOCHIGOME ZU/JUN-YOMEZU – 1 tablespoon See also JAPANESE BLACK VINEGAR
 ↣ 1 tablespoon light yellow rice vinegar/komezu (made with rice plus other grains)

▸ 1 tablespoon brown rice vinegar/*genmaizu* (darker color)

▸ 1 tablespoon distilled rice vinegar/*kokumotsu-su* or part synthetic rice vinegar/*gohseisu* (lower cost grain vinegars)

▸ 1 tablespoon organic rice wine vinegar, such as Ka-Me brand

▸ 1 tablespoon white balsamic vinegar

▸ 2 teaspoon Chinese white rice vinegar (or cider vinegar) plus 1/4 teaspoon water (sharper flavor)

JAPANESE RICE VINEGAR, SEASONED/AWASEZU/SUSHIZU/ YAMABUKUSU – 1 cup

▸ 1 cup white rice vinegar plus 1 tablespoon sugar and 1 teaspoon salt; alternatively, use 2 tablespoons sugar and omit the salt

JAPANESE RICE WINE/CHŎNGJU – 2 tablespoons *See also SAKÉ*

▸ 2 tablespoons dry white vermouth

JAPANESE SEA SALT/ARAJIO (coarse natural sea salt) – 1 tablespoon

▸ 1 teaspoon coarse grain moist French sea salt/*sel gris Marin/sel gris de Guérande*

JAPANESE SEASONED SOUP BASE/MEMMI – 1 generous tablespoon

▸ 1 tablespoon Japanese soy sauce, 1 teaspoon unseasoned rice vinegar, 1/2 teaspoon sugar, and 1/4 teaspoon Asian fish sauce

▸ 1 to 2 tablespoons Japanese light or dark soy sauce

JAPANESE SEAWEED *See ARAME; HIJIKI; KOMBU; MOZUKU; NORI; WAKAME*

JAPANESE SESAME PASTE/NERI-GOMA *See SESAME PASTE*

JAPANESE SEVEN-SPICE SEASONING/SHICHIMI TOGARASHI – 1 teaspoon

▸ 1 teaspoon *nanami-togarashi* (more citrusy tasting)

▸ 3/4 teaspoon ground Japanese chili/*ichimi togarashi* or Chinese ground red pepper (for heat only; lacks flavor)

JAPANESE SOBA DIPPING SAUCE/SOBA-TSUYU See TEMPURA DIPPING SAUCE

JAPANESE SOBA FLOUR/KISOBA (100% pure buckwheat flour) – 1 cup
- ☞ 1 cup fine buckwheat flour or stone-ground buckwheat flour, such as Cold Mountain

JAPANESE SOFT FLOUR/HAKURIK-KO (for cakes and batter) – 1 cup
- ☞ 1 cup cornstarch

JAPANESE SOY SAUCE/SHOYU See SOY SAUCE, JAPANESE

JAPANESE SQUASH See HOKKAIDO; KABOCHA

JAPANESE SUSHI VINEGAR/KASUZU – 1 cup
- ☞ 1 cup Japanese seasoned rice vinegar/*awasezu/sushizu*
- ☞ 1 cup red sushi vinegar/*kasuzu/akazu*

JAPANESE SWEETENER See MIZUAME

JAPANESE SWEET POTATO See JAPANESE MOUNTAIN YAM

JAPANESE SWEET RICE/MOCHI KOME) See RICE, STICKY/SWEET/ GLUTINOUS

JAPANESE SWEET RICE FLOUR/MOCHICO See RICE FLOUR, SWEET/ GLUTINOUS

JAPANESE SWEET RICE WINE See MIRIN

JAPANESE SWEET VINEGAR SEASONING SAUCE/AMAZU – 1/2 cup
Make Your Own Gently heat 1/2 cup rice vinegar, 3 tablespoons granulated sugar, and 1 1/4 teaspoons sea salt until the sugar dissolves, stirring occasionally; cool to room temperature.
Or

Gently heat 1/4 cup each rice vinegar and water, and 1 1/2 tablespoons granulated sugar until the sugar dissolves, stirring occasionally; cool to room temperature (for sunomono or cucumber salad).

JAPANESE TEMPURA BATTER *See TEMPURA BATTER*

JAPANESE TEMPURA DIPPING SAUCE *See TEMPURA DIPPING SAUCE*

JAPANESE TEMPURA FLOUR *See TEMPURA FLOUR*

JAPANESE TERIYAKI SAUCE *See TERIYAKI SAUCE*

JAPANESE TONKATSU SAUCE *See TONKATSU SAUCE*

JAPANESE TORIGARA BASE/WEIHA *See TORIGARA BASE/WEIHA*

JAPANESE TURNIPS/TOKYO TURNIPS/HAKUREI/KABU – 1 POUND
- 1 pound young sweet turnips, peeled and cut into quarters or into spheres with a melon baller
- 1 pound mild globe radishes
- 1 pound French Breakfast or White Icicle radishes, cut in pieces

JAPANESE YAKITORI SAUCE *See YAKITORI SAUCE*

JAPANESE YUKARI SHISO SALT – 1 tablespoon
- 1 tablespoon matcha salt (powdered green tea salt)
- 1 tablespoon seasoning for rice/*furikake See also FURIKAKE*

JASMINE/MALI HORM (Southeast Asian flavoring agent) – 2 tablespoons:
- 2 tablespoons rose petals

JASMINE RICE *See RICE, THAI JASMINE*

JICÀI/SHEPHERD'S PURSE/CAPSELLA BURSA-PASTORIS (salad herb and Asian green vegetable) – 1 pound

- 1 pound mustard greens, green chard, or spinach
- 1 pound pennycress leaves/*Thlaspi arvense,* or wild mustard leaves/ *Brassica rapa* or *B. nigra*

JUJUBES/NATSUME/DAUCHU (Chinese red dates) – 1 cup

- 1 cup canned jujubes, drained (for fresh)
- 1 cup hard crisp apple chunks (for fresh)
- 1/2 cup dried jujubes, softened in cold water 30 minutes (for fresh)
- 1 cup dried goji berries/wolfberries (for dried)
- 1 cup cut up dried dates, dried figs, or prunes (for dried)

K

KABOCHA/NAN GUA (Japanese small, orange flesh winter squash) – 1 pound
- ☞ 1 pound autumn cup, buttercup, butternut, large acorn, golden nugget, or baby Hubbard squash (contains more moisture)

KABOSU (Japanese acidic citrus fruit) – 1
- ☞ 2 Key limes or 1 Persian lime

KABURA (giant Japanese turnip) – 1 pound
- ☞ 1 pound daikon radish

KAFFIR LIME LEAF/WILD LIME LEAF/BAI MAKRUT/DAUN JERUK PURUT, FRESH (Southeast Asian) – 1 leaf
- ☞ 2 thawed frozen kaffir leaves, or 4 reconstituted dried leaves
- ☞ 1/4 teaspoon kaffir lime leaf powder
- ☞ 1 young, fresh organic lemon or lime leaf
- ☞ 1 (3/4-inch) strip of kaffir or lime zest; or 1/4 to 1/2 teaspoon finely grated kaffir or lime zest (added toward the end of cooking)

KAFFIR LIME LEAF POWDER/KAFFIR POWDER – 1 teaspoon
- ☞ 4 or 5 dried kaffir lime leaves, chopped, then ground to a fine powder

KAFFIR LIME JUICE (Southeast Asian) – 1 tablespoon
- ☞ 1 tablespoon sour, unripe Persian lime juice

KAFFIR LIME ZEST, FRESH, FROZEN, OR BRINED – 1 teaspoon finely grated
- ☞ 2 teaspoons dried zest soaked in water to rehydrate (discard soaking water)
- ☞ 1 to 2 tablespoons shredded kaffir lime leaves

☞ 1 1/2 teaspoons finely grated fresh citron or Persian lime zest

KALAMANSI *See CALAMONDIN*

KALAUNJI/KALONJI *See NIGELLA SEEDS*

KANZURI (Japanese fermented chili paste) – 1 teaspoon
  ☞ 1 teaspoon green yuzu chili paste/*yuzu koshu*
  ☞ 1 or 2 drops chili oil

KASHMIRI RED CHILI POWDER (colorful Indian spice) – 1 generous tablespoon
  ☞ 1 tablespoon sweet Hungarian paprika and 1 teaspoon ground cayenne pepper
  ☞ 1 tablespoon hot Hungarian paprika

KATAKURIKO (Japanese starch/thickening agent) – 1 tablespoon
  ☞ 1 tablespoon cornstarch or glutinous sweet rice flour
  ☞ 4 teaspoons arrowroot powder
  ☞ 2 teaspoons instant mashed potato flakes

KATSUOBUSHI *See FISH FLAKES, DRIED*

KECAP ASIN (Indonesian soy sauce) – 1 tablespoon
  ☞ 1 tablespoon Chinese light soy sauce or Maggi Seasoning

KECAP MANIS/KETJAP MANIS (Indonesian sweet, thick soy sauce) – 1/3 cup
  ☞ 1/3 cup Thai sweet black soy sauce/*see-eu wan*
  ☞ 1/3 cup Chinese double dark/double black sweet soy sauce/*yewn she jiang*
  ☞ 1/4 cup Maggi Seasoning plus 1 1/2 tablespoons unsulphured molasses

Make your own Place in a small saucepan 3 tablespoons Chinese dark soy sauce or Japanese tamari, 2 packed tablespoons palm or dark brown sugar, plus a pinch of garlic powder and star anise (if available). Gently heat until the sugar melts (or microwave on High for 20 seconds); stir to mix.

KELP STOCK See *DASHI, VEGETARIAN/KOMBU DASHI; KOMBU STOCK*

KENARI NUT/PILI NUT/PHILIPPINE NUT (Southeast Asian) – 1 cup
- ⮞ 1 cup almonds

KEWRA/KEORA/KEVDA ESSENCE (Sri Lankan and Indian flavoring agent) – 1 or 2 drops
- ⮞ 1/2 or 1 teaspoon kewra (screwpine) water or rose water
- ⮞ 1/2 teaspoon pandan powder or paste (will add green color)
- ⮞ 1 or 2 drops food-grade pure rose extract/essence
- ⮞ 1/4 to 1/2 teaspoon Tahitian vanilla extract
- ⮞ 1- or 2-inch section Tahitian vanilla bean, split lengthwise and seeds scraped out (use the bean and the seeds)

KHICHIYA (Indian popped rice) – 1 cup
- ⮞ 1 cup crisped rice cereal

KHOA/KHOYA/MAWA (East Indian unsweetened solid condensed milk) – 1 cup crumbled
- ⮞ 5 cups full-fat milk heated until reduced to 1 cup, stirring constantly, about 30 minutes
- ⮞ 3/4 cup full-fat dried milk powder

KIKURAGE See *CLOUD EAR/BLACK TREE FUNGUS*

KIMCHI/KIMCHEE/BAECHU KIMCHI (Korean pickled napa cabbage) – 1 cup
- ⮞ 1 cup rinsed and drained sauerkraut plus 1 or 2 teaspoons Korean chili bean paste, such as *gochujang or taeyangcho*, stirred until combined

KIMCHI PASTE/GOCHUJANG/TAEYANGCHO See *KOREAN CHILI BEAN PASTE*

KING OYSTER/ROYAL TRUMPET MUSHROOM – 8 ounces
- 8 ounces fresh white chanterelle, shiitake or matsutake mushrooms
- 4 ounces canned oyster, matsutake, or straw mushrooms

KINOKO (Japanese roasted soybean flour) – 1/4 cup:
- 1/4 cup soybean flour toasted in a small pan over medium heat until slightly darker in color, 4 to 5 minutes

KINOME/PRICKLY ASH LEAF SPRIGS, FRESH (Japanese garnish) – 2 tablespoons
- 2 tablespoons small sprigs of watercress, flat-leaf parsley, cilantro, or mint (for the color)

KOKUM/COCUM (Indian and Malaysian souring agent) – 1-inch by 1/2-inch dried slice
- 1 dried tamarind slice/*asam gelugor/asam jawa*
- 1 tablespoon tamarind pulp or paste/*asam jara*
- 1 tablespoon green mango powder/*amchur* (add toward the end of cooking)
- 1 1/2 tablespoons fresh lemon or lime juice (use 1/2 teaspoon for each segment or broken piece)

KOMATSUNA (Japanese mustard spinach) – 8 ounces
- 8 ounces spinach or mustard greens

KOMBU/DRIED KELP/KONBU/DASHIMA/HAI DAI (dried edible seaweed) – 1/2 ounce
- 1/2 ounce wakame, winged kelp, or sea girdle/finger kombu (milder flavor)
- 1/2 ounce whole leaf digitata kelp/oarweed (tougher; sweeter flavor)

☞ 1/2 ounce dulse, digitata, or wakame flakes/granules (for dashi/ stock, or added at the beginning for cooking grains or beans)

KOMBU CRISPS
Make Your Own Break 4 or 5 strips of kombu into 1-inch pieces and fry in 350°F oil until crisp, 1 to 2 minutes.

KOMBU POWDER (Japanese condiment)
Make Your Own Cut dried kombu into small pieces and toast in a dry skillet, stirring constantly, until very crisp, about 5 minutes. Grind to a coarse powder in a spice/coffee grinder or with a mortar and pestle (or rolling pin).

KOMBU STOCK/KOMBU DASHI-JIRU (Japanese) – 1 cup See also
DASHI, VEGETARIAN
☞ 1-inch strip (1/8 ounce) dried kiri kombu/kelp (or kombu strands/ natto kombu), soaked in 1 cup cold water 8 to 12 hours, then strained (discard the kombu)
☞ 1 1/2 teaspoons dulse flakes brought just to boiling in 1 cup water (or water from soaking dried mushrooms); removed from heat; cooled 5 minutes, then strained
☞ 1 teaspoon powdered kombu dissolved in 1 cup hot water

KOREAN BLACK BEAN PASTE/CHUN JANG See BLACK BEAN SAUCE/
PASTE

KOREAN BROWN RICE VINEGAR/HYUNMI SIKCHO – 1 tablespoon
☞ 1 tablespoon cider vinegar

KOREAN CHILI BEAN PASTE/RED PEPPER PASTE/HOT PEPPER PASTE/
GOCHUJANG – 1 tablespoon
☞ 1 tablespoon Chinese or Sichuan chili bean paste/*dou ban jiang* plus 1 teaspoon molasses
☞ 1 tablespoon Japanese red miso/*inaka/sendai* plus 1/2 teaspoon each corn syrup (or sugar) and ground cayenne pepper

☞ 1/2 tablespoon each Japanese white miso/*shiro/saikyo* and Asian red chili sauce, such as sambal oelek, plus 1/2 teaspoon molasses

KOREAN CHILI FLAKES/COARSE RED PEPPER POWDER/KOCHUKARU – 1 teaspoon

☞ 1 teaspoon Chinese coarsely ground chili/*la jiao mian*
☞ 1 teaspoon mild chili powder, such as ancho, California or New Mexico (for chili powder)
☞ 3/4 teaspoon crushed red pepper flakes (for chili flakes)

KOREAN CHILI THREADS/SILGOCHU

☞ Mild, red, deseeded chilis, flattened and wrapped in a damp paper towel; left an hour to soften, then rolled and sliced into 2- to 3-inch-long threads

KOREAN DIPPING SAUCE – 3 tablespoons See also KOREAN SESAME PASTE DIPPING SAUCE

☞ 1 tablespoon unseasoned rice vinegar and 2 tablespoons reduced-sodium soy sauce, stirred until combined

KOREAN FERMENTED BEAN AND CHILI SAUCE/SSÄMJANG – 3 tablespoons

☞ 1 tablespoon soybean paste/*doenjang* stirred into 2 tablespoons chili bean paste/*gochujang/taeyangcho*

KOREAN FERMENTED BEAN PASTE/DOENJANG See KOREAN SOYBEAN PASTE

KOREAN FISH SAUCE/SAENGSEON SAUCE See FISH SAUCE

KOREAN GRAIN SYRUP/MALT SYRUP/JOCHEONG/CHOCHONG/MUL YUT – 1 cup

☞ 1 cup light-colored corn syrup

KOREAN GREEN PEPPER/KOCHU – 1

☞ 1 large green jalapeño chili

☞ 1 peeled green bell pepper or Anaheim chili (for mild green pepper)

KOREAN LEEK/DAEPA – 1
☞ 1 large scallion or green/spring onion

KOREAN MUSHROOMS/PYOGA See SHIITAKE MUSHROOMS

KOREAN NOODLES, BUCKWHEAT AND SWEET POTATO STARCH/ NAENG MYUN – 8 ounces
☞ 8 ounces buckwheat noodles/*soba/memil guksu*, green tea soba/ *cha soba*, or thin soba/*ki soba*
☞ 8 ounces Italian whole-wheat spaghetti, spaghettini, or vermicelli

KOREAN NOODLES, SWEET POTATO OR MUNG BEAN STARCH/DANG MYUN – 8 ounces
☞ 8 ounces Chinese cellophane/bean thread noodles/*fen si/sei fun*
☞ 8 ounces Japanese bean thread vermicelli/*harusame*
☞ 8 ounces Thai clear transparent noodles/*wun sen*
☞ 8 ounces Vietnamese mung bean noodles/*bun tau*
☞ 8 ounces Filipino cellophane noodles/*sotánghon*

KOREAN NOODLES, THICK WHEAT/NAMA/JAJANG MYUN, FRESH OR DRIED – 8 ounces
☞ 8 ounces fresh or dried Korean *kalguksu* noodles, or fresh or dried Japanese udon noodles

KOREAN NOODLES, THIN WHEAT/SOMYUN/GOUGSOU, DRIED – 8 ounces
☞ 8 ounces dried Japanese *somen* or *hiyamugi* noodles, Filipino *miswa* noodles, or Indian *misoa* noodles
☞ 8 ounces dried angel hair pasta, spaghettini, or fine vermicelli

KOREAN PICKLED CABBAGE/KIMCHI See KIMCHI

KOREAN RADISH/MU See DAIKON

KOREAN RED PEPPER FLAKES *See KOREAN CHILI FLAKES*

KOREAN RED PEPPER THREADS *See KOREAN CHILI THREADS*

KOREAN RICE *See RICE, KOREAN*

KOREAN RICE LIQUOR/SOJU – 1 tablespoon
- 1 tablespoon Japanese sweet rice cooking wine/*mirin*
- 1 tablespoon Chinese yellow rice cooking wine/*michiu/mi jiu*
- 1/2 teaspoon sugar or honey dissolved in 1 tablespoon white wine, saké, vermouth, sherry, or water
- 1 tablespoon vodka

KOREAN RICE WINE/CHUNG-JU/YAKJU – 1/4 cup
- 1/4 cup Chinese yellow rice wine/Shaoxing/Shao Hsing, or medium-dry sherry, such as amontillado

KOREAN ROASTED BARLEY TEA/BORICHA – 1/4 cup
Make Your Own Toast 1/4 cup pearl barley in a dry skillet over medium heat, stirring occasionally, until brown and fragrant, 10 to 15 minutes.

KOREAN SESAME PASTE DIPPING SAUCE/GGAE GANJANG – 1/4 cup
Make Your Own Toast 1/4 cup hulled (white) sesame seeds in a dry skillet over medium heat, stirring constantly, until golden brown, about 2 minutes. Immediately pour onto a plate to prevent overbrowning. Crush the seeds with a mortar and pestle and then add 1 tablespoon soy sauce, 1 tablespoon unseasoned rice vinegar, and 1 1/2 teaspoons sugar and mix well. Store in an airtight container in the refrigerator. It should last a couple of months.

KOREAN SHRIMP, SALTED/FERMENTED MINI/SAEUJEOT/SAEWOO-JEOT – 1 tablespoon
- 1 tablespoon dried shrimp
- 1 tablespoon Asian fish sauce
- 2 teaspoons Asian fermented shrimp paste

KOREAN SOLAR SALT (coarse, crunchy salt) – 1 tablespoon
  ↠ 1 tablespoon kosher salt

KOREAN SOYBEAN PASTE/DOENJANG – 1 tablespoon
  ↠ 1 tablespoon Japanese red miso/*inaka*/*sendai* or brown miso/*hatcho* (less salty; smoother texture)

KOREAN SOY SAUCE See SOY SAUCE, KOREAN

KOREAN SWEET RICE FLOUR/CHAPSSALGARU See FLOUR, SWEET/ GLUTINOUS RICE

KOREAN WATERCRESS/MINARI – 1 cup
  ↠ 1 cup fresh garden cress stems or flat-leaf parsley stems

KRACHAI See FINGERROOT

KYOHO GRAPES (Japanese) – 1 pound
  ↠ 1 pound Concord grapes

KYONA See MIZUNA, EARLY

L

LAKSA LEAF See *VIETNAMESE MINT*

LAKSA NOODLES/LEI FUN, FRESH (Singaporean and Malaysian) – 1 pound
- 8 ounces dried Filipino pancit noodles, or other thick white rice noodles, prepared according to the package directions
- 8 to 12 ounces dried Shanghai noodles or spaghetti (contains wheat), prepared according to the package directions

LAOS POWDER (ground galangal root) – 1 teaspoon See also *GALANGAL, GREATER*
- 1/2 inch peeled and finely minced galangal (fresh, frozen, or brined)
- 1 or 2 small (1/8-inch) slices dried galangal root/*galanga* (add whole to soup or stock without soaking)
- 1 1/2 teaspoons grated fresh ginger plus a few grains of ground black pepper, or a few drops of lemon juice

LARD, FRESH LEAF (rendered pork fat) – 1 cup
- 1 cup beef tallow (rendered beef fat)
- 3/4 cup nonhydrogenated solid vegetable shortening plus 1/4 cup chilled strained bacon drippings
- 1 cup plus 1 1/2 tablespoons supermarket lard or nonhydrogenated solid vegetable shortening
- 1 cup clarified unsalted butter or ghee
- 1 cup peanut oil plus 1 teaspoon clarified/strained bacon drippings (for frying)
- 1 cup clarified/strained bacon, poultry, or meat fat/drippings; or mild virgin olive oil (for sautéing/shallow frying, not deep fat frying)
Make Your Own Grind or finely chop 12 ounces semi-frozen unsalted pork fatback (or fat trimmed from pork shoulder without any traces of meat). Melt it in a large, heavy skillet in a preheated 200°F to 225°F

oven (or with 1/4 cup water on the lowest possible stovetop setting) for 1 to 1 1/2 hours. Strain in a cheesecloth-lined sieve and cool until solid. (It will be softer than leaf lard rendered from kidney fat.)

LEAVES FOR WRAPPING AND STEAMING *See WRAPPERS FOR FOOD, VEGETABLE-BASED*

LEEK ROOT/INDIAN LEEK/JUMYIT *See CHINESE CHIVES*

LEMON BASIL/BAI MANGLAEK/KEMANGIE, FRESH – 1 ounce
- 1 ounce fresh lime basil (darker leaves; lime aroma)
- 1 ounce fresh sweet basil (Italian, French, or California) plus a little lemon balm or lemon zest

LEMONGRASS, FRESH – 3- to 5-inch trimmed bottom third of inner core/1 to 3 tablespoons finely chopped
- 2 tablespoons frozen lemongrass slices (if home-frozen, slice thinly while frozen)
- 1 to 1 1/2 tablespoons crumbled or shredded freeze-dried lemongrass soaked in 1 to 1 1/2 tablespoons water until softened, 15 to 20 minutes
- 2 teaspoons oil-packed lemongrass, blotted dry
- 1 teaspoon sereh/serai powder (lemongrass powder)
- 1 or 2 teaspoons lemongrass paste/puree
- 2 tablespoons chopped lemon leaves or lemon verbena leaves (added at the last moment)
- 2 teaspoons chopped lemon balm or lemon myrtle leaves (added at the last moment)
- 2 (1-inch) strips lemon peel (white pith scraped away) blanched in boiling water 2 or 3 seconds, then blotted dry
- 1 teaspoon finely grated lemon zest

LEMON OIL/DAU CHANH (Asian flavoring agent) – 1/3 cup
Make Your Own Combine 1/3 cup vegetable oil with 1 tablespoon lemon zest from a well-scrubbed lemon (preferably organic) and heat

slowly until small bubbles appear, 7 to 10 minutes. Cool and strain; store, tightly covered, in the refrigerator; it will last for up to 1 week.

LENGKUAS (Indonesian and Malaysian seasoning) *See GALANGAL, GREATER*

LILY BUDS/GOLDEN NEEDLES/GUM JUM/JIN ZHEN/CAI KIM CHAM/ WONCHURI, DRIED (Asian seasoning and garnish)
- ☞ Yellow, unopened common daylily/*Hemerocallis fulva* flower buds, dried in a warm, airy place until brittle, about 7 days (To rehydrate, soak in warm water 30 minutes, then trim off the fibrous end bit.)
- ☞ Finely shredded green cabbage (for texture; lacks taste)

LILY BULB/TIGER LILY BULB/LILIUM TIGRINUM/BOCK HUP/YURINE/ BAI HE, FRESH OR VACUUM PACKED (Asian vegetable) – 1/2 cup chopped
- ☞ 1/2 cup chopped canned bamboo shoots, rinsed and drained
- ☞ 1/2 cup small salad turnips, such as Hakurei or Tokyo Market
- ☞ 1/2 cup chopped white-fleshed sweet potatoes, such as Cuba, boniato, or yampi

LIME, KAFFIR *See KAFFIR*

LIME, RANGPUR, JUICE – 1 tablespoon
- ☞ 2 teaspoons Key or Persian lime juice and 1 teaspoon tangerine juice

LIME, RANGPUR, ZEST – 1 teaspoon
- ☞ 1 teaspoon Key lime, tangerine, or tangelo zest

LIME, SWEET/LIMO/NARAN-KAI/SOM KLEANG (mild-tasting citrus fruit) – 1
- ☞ 1 Meyer lemon

LIME, THAI/MANAO, JUICE – 1 tablespoon
- ☞ 1 tablespoon Key lime juice plus a dash of Meyer lemon juice

LIME, THAI/MANO ZEST – 1 teaspoon
- 1 teaspoon Key lime zest

LONG PEPPER, INDONESIAN/INDIAN/DIPPLI/TIEU LOP (Indian and Southeast Asian seasoning) – 1 tablespoon
- 1 tablespoon dried Tasmanian pepperberries or Szechuan peppercorns (red colored)
- 1 tablespoon white peppercorns or 2 teaspoons black peppercorns

LOQUATS, FRESH (small, sweet-sour yellow fruits) – 1 pound
- 1 (15-ounce) can loquats, drained
- 1 pound fresh acerola or apricots

LOTUS LEAVES, MATURE/DRIED See WRAPPERS FOR FOOD, NON-EDIBLE

LOTUS ROOT/ŎU/RENKON/HASU/LEEN NGOW (crisp Asian vegetable) – 1 (5-inch) section/7 to 8 ounces/1 cup peeled and sliced
- 1 cup sliced frozen lotus root
- 1 cup sliced fresh lotus stems/rootlets/*ngo sen*
- 1 cup sliced canned lotus root, rinsed under cold water (light gray in color; best in a soy sauce–based dish)
- 1/2 cup sliced, unbleached, dried lotus root soaked in cool water for 2 hours (or 20 minutes in hot water) then drained
- 1 cup peeled and sliced fresh water chestnuts (blanch for 5 minutes to make peeling easier)
- 1 cup scrubbed and sliced Chinese artichokes/crosnes or young Jerusalem artichokes/sunchokes

LOTUS ROOT FLOUR/STARCH/ŎU FEN (Chinese thickening and dredging agent) – 1 tablespoon
- 1 tablespoon cornstarch, kudzu powder, or water chestnut starch/powder

LOTUS ROOTLETS/STEMS/NGO SEN (Southeast Asian vegetable) – 1 cup
- 1 cup jarred brined lotus rootlets, rinsed under cold water

☞ 1 cup thinly sliced peeled lotus root

LOTUS SEEDS, DRIED/MAKHANA/HOT SEN KHO/LIEN JEE/MED BUA – 1/2 cup
☞ 1 cup canned lotus seeds or canned whole hominy, drained and rinsed

LUMPIA WRAPPERS (Filipino pastry wrappers) – 8 wrappers
☞ 8 frozen, super-thin spring roll wrappers (thaw before separating)
☞ 8 Shanghai-style egg roll wrappers
☞ 8 ounces dried Vietnamese rice paper wrappers (individually soften in hot water until pliable)
☞ 8 ounces phyllo pastry cut to size (thinner, more delicate)

Make Your Own Blend or process 2/3 cup cornstarch, 1 egg, 1/2 cup plus 2 tablespoons water, and a pinch of salt until smooth; let sit for 15 minutes. Working with 1 1/2 tablespoons batter at a time, cook in a preheated, lightly oiled nonstick skillet about 1 1/2 minutes, spreading out the batter with a spoon to about 6 inches in diameter. Place on a plate and keep covered with a damp towel while you make the rest. They will keep in the refrigerator for a day or two or frozen for a few months.

LYCHEE HONEY – 1 cup
☞ 1 cup clover honey, or other mild, fragrant golden honey

LYCHEES/LITCHIS, FRESH – 1 bunch (about 20), peeled and seeded
☞ 2 ounces dried lychees softened in warm water
☞ 1 (20-ounce) can lychees/litchis, rambutans, or longans, drained
☞ 20 fresh or frozen pulasans, rambutans, or longans, peeled and seeded
☞ 20 large fresh grapes, such as Red Globe, Tokay, or Muscat, seeded and peeled

M

MACAPUNO COCONUT STRINGS (Filipino jarred sweet coconut in syrup) – 1 cup
- ☞ 1 cup sweetened shredded coconut

MACE/JAVITRI/DAWK JAN (flavoring spice) – 1 mace blade (1 teaspoon crumbled/flakes)
- ☞ 1/2 teaspoon ground mace
- ☞ 1 scant teaspoon freshly grated nutmeg, or 1/2 teaspoon fine-ground nutmeg
- ☞ 1/2 teaspoon ground allspice

MADAN/GARCINIA (Southeast Asian small sour, crisp fruit) – 1
- ☞ 1 unripe green plum or nectarine

MAIDA (Indian finely-milled wheat flour) – 1 cup
- ☞ 1 cup cake flour

MAITAKE MUSHROOMS – 1 pound
- ☞ 1 pound shiitake or oyster/shimeji mushrooms

MALABAR SPINACH/CEYLON SPINACH/BASELLA ALBA/LO KUI/MONG TOI/SAAN CHOY/PUI SHAAG – 1 pound
- ☞ 1 pound sweet potato leaves/*Ipomoea batata* (not regular potato leaves, which are poisonous)
- ☞ 1 pound tender young mallow leaves/*Malva neglecta*
- ☞ 1 pound mature spinach, Chinese spinach, or green chard (no mucilaginous properties)
- ☞ 2 teaspoons filé powder/dried sassafras leaves (for a mucilaginous agent; add it to the dish after removing from heat)

MALAI (Indian cooking cream) – 1 cup
 ⊨ 1 cup English clotted cream or Lebanese ashtar

MALDIVE FISH/UMBALAKADA (Sri Lankan cooking condiment) – 1 tablespoon pounded, flaked or powdered
 ⊨ 1 tablespoon coarsely chopped dried shrimp, or 1 1/2 tablespoons shrimp powder/floss
 ⊨ 1 or 2 tablespoons bonito flakes/*katsuobushi*, crumbled to a powder
 ⊨ 1 tablespoon flaked or crumbled dried cod

MANGO, GREEN/KACHA AM, FRESH OR FROZEN (Indian and Southeast Asian souring and tenderizing agent) – 1 medium (1 pound)
 ⊨ 1/3 cup *amchur* slices (sun-dried green mango) soaked in hot water until softened, 30 to 60 minutes
 ⊨ 1 hard green unripe yellow/eating mango plus a few drops lime juice (wear plastic gloves when handling raw green mango)
 ⊨ 1/4 of a green papaya
 ⊨ 1 large unpeeled green tart cooking apple, such as Granny Smith or Bramley's Seedling, soaked in acidulated water after cutting, then patted dry

MANGO POWDER, GREEN See AMCHOOR/AMCHUR

MANGO PUREE, FRESH OR FROZEN – 1 cup
 ⊨ 1 cup canned Alphonso mango pulp (or Kesar variety for Indian dishes)
 ⊨ 2 fresh ripe Alphonso or Ataulfo mangos, peeled and pureed

MANGO, RIPE, FRESH – 1 cup sliced
 ⊨ 1 cup thawed frozen mango chunks, halves, or puree
 ⊨ 1 cup drained canned mango chunks
 ⊨ 1/2 cup unsweetened dried mango slices soaked in warm water until softened, about 4 hours
 ⊨ 1 cup canned Alphonso mango pulp (for desserts and drinks)

☞ 1 cup sliced Hawaiian papaya or very sweet cantaloupe

MANTOU (fluffy, steamed Chinese buns made with wheat flour) See *CHINESE STEAMED BUNS*

MATCHA/MACCHA/HIKI-CHA (Japanese culinary-grade green tea powder)
- ☞ Japanese Sencha green tea, ground and pressed through a fine-mesh sieve, then spread on parchment paper to dry, about 1 hour (less colorful)
- ☞ Green food coloring powder (for baking; use following package directions; less flavorful)

MATSUTAKE/JAPANESE PINE MUSHROOM – 8 ounces
- ☞ 8 ounces fresh albarelle, blewit/blue foot, oyster, or shiitake mushrooms
- ☞ 4 ounces canned matsutake or nameko mushrooms, drained

MATSUTAKE POWDER (Dried mushroom powder) – 1 tablespoon
- ☞ 1 tablespoon porcini powder (or dried porcini mushrooms ground in a spice/coffee grinder)

MEJISO (Japanese seedlings garnish) See *SHOOTS AND SPROUTS*

MELINJO/BELINJO NUTS (Indonesian soup addition) – 1/4 cup
- ☞ 1/4 cup raw peanuts

MIRIN/HON-MIRIN (Japanese sweetened rice cooking wine containing 14% alcohol, or 8% if sold in the United States) – 1 tablespoon
- ☞ 1 tablespoon *aji no haha mirin* (more like sake; contains 10% alcohol)
- ☞ 1 tablespoon *shin-mirin* or *mirin-fuhmi*) (synthetic mirin; contains 1% alcohol)
- ☞ 1 tablespoon Mirin Style Seasoning (contains 0.12% alcohol)
- ☞ 1 1/2 tablespoon *aji-mirin* (contains sweetener and salt)

- ☞ 2 tablespoons each saké and granulated sugar gently simmered until the sugar dissolves, and the liquid is reduced by half
- ☞ 1 teaspoon sugar dissolved in 1 tablespoon saké or sweet sherry
- ☞ 2 teaspoons sugar (or 1 teaspoon honey) dissolved in 1 tablespoon unseasoned rice wine vinegar, white wine, vermouth, or hot water

MISO, DARK/KURO/MUGI/ INAKA/SENDAI/ HATCHO (Japanese red or dark brown fermented soybean-based paste) – 1 tablespoon

- ☞ 1/2 teaspoon beef bouillon (stock) granules or 1/2 beef bouillon cube
- ☞ 2 teaspoons Chinese fermented black beans/*dow see,* rinsed
- ☞ 1 tablespoon fermented soybean paste: Chinese *dou jiang,* Korean *doenjang,* or Filipino *tausi*
- ☞ 1 tablespoon hoisin sauce
- ☞ 1 tablespoon light miso plus 1 teaspoon dark soy sauce
- ☞ 2 teaspoons anchovy paste
- ☞ 2 teaspoons tomato paste and 1 teaspoon soy sauce
- ☞ 1 teaspoon Japanese organic whole-bean soy sauce/*marudaizu shoyu,* organic tamari, or other thick soy sauce
- ☞ 1 teaspoon yeast extract spread, such as Marmite or Vegemite

MISO, GLUTEN-FREE – 1 tablespoon

- ☞ 1 tablespoon rice *kome* miso, brown rice *genmai* miso, garbanzo bean miso, soybean *hatcho* miso, or golden millet miso

MISO, LIGHT/SHIRO/SHINSHU/SAIKYO (Japanese mild white or yellow fermented soybean-based paste) – 1 tablespoon

- ☞ 1 tablespoon (or more) low-sodium saikyo miso (contains 5% salt)
- ☞ 1 tablespoon *awase* miso (a mixture of white and red miso)
- ☞ 1 tablespoon Chinese yellow soybean paste/*hugan jian,* Vietnamese *tuong ot,* or Thai *tao jiaw*
- ☞ 1 1/2 teaspoons anchovy paste and 1/2 teaspoon tahini or sesame butter/paste
- ☞ 1/2 scant teaspoon coarse sea salt

MISO, SOY-FREE – 1 tablespoon
 ▹ 1 tablespoon azuki miso, chickpea miso, or sweet brown rice miso

MITSUBA/JAPANESE PARSLEY/JAPANESE CHERVIL/TREFOIL, FRESH – 1 chopped tablespoon
 ▹ 2 teaspoons chopped fresh Italian flat-leaf parsley and 1 teaspoon chopped fresh celery leaves (for seasoning)
 ▹ 1 tablespoon chopped fresh cilantro or parsley (for garnish)
 ▹ 1 tablespoon watercress sprigs or daikon sprouts/*kaiware* (for garnish)
 ▹ 1 tablespoon chervil, or young stems and leafy tops of honewort/wild chervil/*Cryptotaenia canadensis*

MIYOGA See MYOGA/GINGER BUD

MIYUK (Korean sun-dried kelp) See KOMBU; SEAWEED

MIZUAME/WATER CANDY (Japanese starch-based sweetener/syrup) – 1/4 cup
 ▹ Scant 1/3 cup light-colored (not "lite") corn syrup, brought to a full boil then cooled
 ▹ 2 tablespoons pale, mild-tasting honey (such as clover or alfalfa)
 ▹ 2 tablespoons golden syrup (adds color)

MIZUNA, EARLY/SPIDER MUSTARD/KYONA/SIU CAI (Japanese mustard greens) – 1 ounce (1 cup)
 ▹ 1 cup Kyona (wider leaves; stronger peppery flavor)
 ▹ 1 cup mibuna (long, slender leaves; stronger mustard flavor)
 ▹ 1 cup baby arugula, baby mustard greens, young horseradish leaves, or tatsoi
 ▹ 1 cup mustard spinach/*komatsuna,* trimmed and torn into bite-size pieces (milder flavor)
 ▹ 1 cup minutina/*Erba stella* leaves cut into 1 1/2- to 2-inch lengths (milder flavor)

MONGOLIAN FIVE-SPICE POWDER *See CHINESE FIVE-SPICE POWDER*

MOO SHU SHELLS/PANCAKES/SKINS/PEKING DOILIES (Chinese wheat flour wrappers) – 1 dozen
- ☞ 1 dozen small, thin flour tortillas; small crepes; or small, paper-thin pancakes

MOZUKU (Japanese seaweed) – 8 ounces fresh
- ☞ 7 ounces canned seaweed salad, drained and rinsed
- ☞ 4 ounces dried mozuku, soaked in water for 1 hour, rinsed, and then scalded with hot water

MUGI/HATO MUGI/COIX LACRYMA–JOBI (Japanese whole-grain barley) – 1 pound
- ☞ 1 pound whole-grain/pot or pearl barley (smaller; slightly different flavor)

MU SHU SAUCE (Chinese condiment) – 1 tablespoon
- ☞ 1 tablespoon hoisin sauce

MUNG BEAN FLOUR/STARCH/POWDER/TEPUNG HOEN KWE/PANG TUA (smooth Asian thickening and cooking flour) – 1 tablespoon
- ☞ 1 tablespoon brown or white rice flour (for pastries)
- ☞ 1 1/2 tablespoons mung beans ground until fine in spice/coffee grinder, then sifted and measured (for thickening)
- ☞ 1 tablespoon arrowroot powder, sweet/glutinous rice flour, or cornstarch (for thickening)

MUNG BEAN SPROUTS – 1 cup (2 ounces)
- ☞ 1 cup regular bean sprouts or sunflower sprouts (smaller, less crunchy)
- ☞ 1 cup Chinese pea sprouts (more delicate)
- ☞ 1 cup soybean sprouts (stronger flavored)
- ☞ 1 cup snow peas trimmed and julienned
- ☞ 1 cup celtuce stems peeled and thinly sliced

MUNG BEANS, YELLOW/SKINNED, SPLIT GREEN MUNG BEAN/DHULI MUNG DAL, DRIED – 1 pound
- 1 pound mung bean sprouts (faster cooking)
- 1 pound adzuki beans/*chori dal* (a little larger)
- 1 pound dried Spanish verdina beans (longer cooking time)
- 1 pound small dried flageolets or pigeon peas (larger)
- 1 cup toasted peanuts

MUSHROOM BROTH – 1 quart
- 1 quart reduced-sodium vegetable broth plus 4 to 8 ounces cut-up mushrooms (portobello, cremini, shiitake) simmered partly covered for 20 to 25 minutes, then strained
- 2 to 3 teaspoons jarred mushroom base added to 1 quart boiling water

MUSHROOM ESSENCE – 1/3 to 1/2 cup
- 1 pound fresh porcini or shiitake mushrooms frozen, thawed, and squeezed to extract the liquid (reserve the juiced mushrooms for another use)
- 1 pound fresh porcini or shiitake mushrooms and 2 cups water cooked for 15 minutes in a covered saucepan; strained, then gently boiled until reduced to one-quarter the volume

MUSHROOM POWDER/POWDERED MUSHROOMS – 2 tablespoons
See also PORCINI POWDER
- 6 tablespoons crumbled dried mushrooms, ground in a spice/coffee grinder or blender until powdery
- 8 ounces fresh mushrooms
- 1 (4-ounce) can whole or sliced mushrooms, drained

MUSHROOM POWDER, WILD – 1 teaspoon
- 1 ounce ground dried mushrooms

MUSHROOM SALT/BOT NEM (Vietnamese seasoning) – 1 teaspoon
- 1/2 teaspoon kosher salt (less flavor)

MUSHROOMS, DRIED – *3 ounces*
- 1 pound fresh mushrooms
- 10 ounces canned mushrooms, drained

Make Your Own Slice 1 pound fresh mushrooms, spread in a single layer on a baking sheet, and dry at 170°F until crisp, about 2 hours, flipping halfway through. Store thoroughly dried mushrooms, tightly sealed, in the refrigerator or freezer for up to 12 months.

MUSTARD GREENS/SARSON *(strong-tasting Indian greens)* – *1 pound:*
- 1 pound arugula, broccoli rabe, escarole (dark outer leaves), purple mizuna, daikon or other radish greens, turnip greens, garland chrysanthemum, or Texsel greens/Abyssianian mustard/*Brassica carinata*
- 1 pound collard greens, kohlrabi greens, parsnip greens, or purple pak choy (milder flavor)
- 1 pound field mustard/wild mustard leaves/*Brassica rapa* or *B. nigra* (smaller leaves; spicier flavor)
- 1 pound garlic mustard leaves/*Alliaria petiolata,* stringy stems discarded (garlic flavor)
- 1 pound wild pennycress leaves/*Thlaspi arvense* (smaller leaves; spicier flavor)

MUSTARD GREENS, SOUR PICKLED/DUA CAI CHUA/PHAK DONG *(Southeast Asian condiment)* – *1/2 cup*
- 1 chopped kosher dill pickle

MUSTARD OIL/MUSTARD SEED OIL/SHORSHER TEL/SARSON KA TAEL *(Indian seasoning)* – *1 tablespoon*
- 1 tablespoon vegetable oil plus 1/4 teaspoon dry mustard (add the powder when adding the recipe's liquid)

MUSTARD SEED, BLACK/RAI *(Indian seasoning)* – *1 tablespoon:*
- 4 teaspoons brown mustard seeds (less pungent)

MUSTARD, CHINESE/PAI-CHIEH – 1 tablespoon

Make Your Own Stir together 1 tablespoon mustard powder (Chinese *gai lat* or European Colman's) and 1 tablespoon cool water to form a paste. Cover and let sit for 15 minutes to develop the flavor.

MUSTARD, JAPANESE/KERASHI – 1 tablespoon

▷ 1 tablespoon Chinese or English prepared hot mustard

Make Your Own Stir together 2 teaspoons Japanese powdered mustard/*koba kerashi*, or Oriental powdered mustard or English mustard powder and 1 tablespoon cold water to form a paste. Cover and let sit for 15 minutes to mellow and develop the flavor.

MYOGA/GINGER BUD/ZINGIBER MIOGA (Japanese and Korean seasoning) – 1 tablespoon shredded

▷ 1 tablespoon minced young ginger with a pinch of minced lemongrass

▷ 1 tablespoon minced scallions with a pinch of grated fresh ginger

▷ 1 tablespoon shredded pickled ginger, rinsed

N

NAARTJIE PEEL, DRIED *See TANGERINE/MANDARIN PEEL, DRIED*

NAGAIMO (Japanese gelatinous white-fleshed tuber) – 1 ounce for thickening (2 tablespoons grated)
- 1 tablespoon cornstarch mixed with 1 tablespoon liquid

NAM PLA *See THAI FISH SAUCE*

NAM PRIK (Thai dipping sauce) – 1/4 cup
- 2 tablespoons fresh lime juice, 1 tablespoon each sugar and Thai fish sauce (*nam pla* or *pla raa*), 1 teaspoon chopped cilantro, and 1 small minced garlic clove (For chili dipping sauce, add 1 or 2 table-spoons minced or sliced fresh Thai chili.)

NAMEKO MUSHROOMS, FRESH – 1 pound
- 10 ounces canned or jarred nameko mushrooms, drained
- 3 ounces dried nameko or shiitake mushrooms, soaked in warm water until softened, 30 to 45 minutes
- 1 pound fresh shiitake mushrooms, stems discarded

NAN/NAAN (Indian white-flour or whole-wheat flatbread) – 1
- 1 pita bread or flour tortilla

NATTO (Japanese fermented soybean condiment) – 1/4 cup
- 1/4 cup fermented black beans or bean paste (less pungent)

NIGELLA SEEDS/KALONJI/KALIJEERA/CHARNUSHKA (Indian seasoning) – 1 teaspoon
- 1 teaspoon ajwain/ajowan seeds, black cumin seeds, black sesame seeds, caraway seeds, or cracked black pepper (for garnish, not taste)

NIHAIZU (Japanese base for dressings and marinades) – 1/4 cup
- 2 tablespoons rice vinegar and Japanese soy sauce; or equal parts rice vinegar, soy sauce, and dashi

NIPA PALM VINEGAR (Filipino 5% acidity vinegar) See PALM VINEGAR

NOODLES See IDIAPPAM; CHINESE EGG NOODLES; CHINESE WHEAT NOODLES; JAPANESE NOODLES; KOREAN NOODLES; THAI NOODLES; VIETNAMESE NOODLES

NOODLES, CELLOPHANE/BEAN THREAD/FEN SI/HARUSAME/ SAIFUN/SOTANGHON/DANGMYUN/WUN SEN/BUN TAU – 8 ounces
- 8 ounces fresh precooked *shirataki* noodles, rinsed and drained
- 8 ounces kelp noodles, rinsed and drained
- 8 ounces fresh raw squash noodles (cut from a spiral slicer; or cut into long flat strips, then stacked and cut into noodle-like ribbons)
- 8 ounces fresh (or 4 ounces dried) rice noodles, rice sticks, or rice vermicelli, prepared according to the package directions

NOODLES, RAMEN, FRESH – 1 (5-ounce) package See also JAPANESE NOODLES, THIN WHEAT EGG
- 5 ounces fresh Chinese egg noodles (lo mein or chow mein noodles)
- 1 (3-ounce) package dried ramen noodles/*chukka soba/chukamen*
- 5 ounces fresh Italian capellini or vermicelli
- 5 ounces shirataki noodles or rice angel hair (gluten-free)

NOODLES, THICK, FLAT WHEAT, FRESH – 1 pound
- 1 pound fresh *pici*, pappardelle, lasagna noodles, or other thick pasta, cut into segments
- 1 pound fresh or thawed frozen wonton or gyoza wrappers, sliced into ribbons

NOODLES, THIN, FLAT RICE, SEMI-DRIED – 8 ounces See also THAI NOODLES
- 6 ounces thin dried rice noodles, soaked an extra 10 minutes

- 8 ounces rice noodle sheets (*sa-ho*) sliced into ribbons
- 8 ounces dried wheat noodles, cooked according to the package directions

NORI/DRIED PURPLE LAVER/HOSHI-NORI/KIM (thin seaweed sheets of dried compressed laver for wrapping sushi and rice balls) – 4 sheets

- 4 sheets pretoasted nori sheets/*yakinori*
- 4 thin, tender blades of rehydrated wakame, giant kelp, or bullwhip kelp
- 4 sheets rice paper/wafer paper
- 8 paper-thin sheets of daikon radish
- 2 soybean wrappers/paper/*mamenori* (thin, pliable soybean sheet; cut whole sheet in half)
- 4 paper-thin fried egg sheets/sweet crepes/*usa yaki tamago* (use 3 eggs, 1/4 teaspoon salt, and 1 teaspoon sugar for 4 (8-inch) crepes)
- Silicone mat, plastic wrap, dampened cotton dishtowel or linen napkin (for forming sushi rolls/*nori-maki* without nori sheets or other edible wrappers)

NORI FLAKES, SHREDS, OR POWDER/AO NORI/AO-NORIKO (Japanese seaweed seasoning and garnish for salads and raw vegetables)

- Nori or wakame sheets, shredded and toasted in a dry skillet for 1 minute, then crushed or ground in a spice/coffee grinder
- Roasted and seasoned nori/*ajitsuke-nori*, or nori with sesame seeds/*nori komi furikake*, shredded
- Powdered sea lettuce/green laver powder
- Buckwhip kelp, lightly crushed

NUOC CHAM See VIETNAMESE SWEET-AND-SOUR DIPPING SAUCE

NUOC NAM See VIETNAMESE FISH SAUCE

NUTMEG, EAST INDIAN/JAIFAL/LUUK JAN (seasoning spice) – 1 teaspoon fine ground

- 2 teaspoons freshly grated East Indian nutmeg

- 1 1/3 teaspoons freshly grated Grenadian West Indian nutmeg
- 2/3 teaspoon fine ground Grenadian West Indian nutmeg
- 3/4 teaspoon crumbled mace blade or 1/2 teaspoon ground mace
- 1 teaspoon ground allspice or cinnamon
- 1 teaspoon apple pie spice or pumpkin pie spice

O

OIL, CURRY *See CURRY OIL*

OKONOMIYAKI SAUCE (Japanese condiment) – 1 tablespoon
- 1 tablespoon tonkatsu sauce or yakisoba sauce

OKRA, FRESH/BAMIA/BHINDI/KRACHIAP/OKURA/VENDAKA (gelatinous vegetable) – 1 pound
- 1 pound purslane leaves, thick stems removed, cut into pieces
- 1 pound nopale/cactus paddles, shaved and sliced
- 1 to 2 pounds young common mallow leaves or stems/*Malva neglecta,* or young Malabar spinach leaves/*Basella alba* (for thickening)
- 1 tablespoon (or more) filé powder/dried sassafras leaves (for thickening; add to the dish just before or after removing from the heat)

ORANGE BLOSSOM WATER *See ORANGE FLOWER WATER*

ORANGE FLOWER WATER/ORANGE BLOSSOM WATER – 1 tablespoon
- 1/2 teaspoon orange extract
- 1/16 to 1/8 teaspoon orange citrus oil, such as Boyajian (double the amount for a cooked dish)
- 2 teaspoons finely grated orange zest
- 1/3 teaspoon Sicilian flower essence/*Fiori di Sicilia* (has vanilla and orange aroma)

Make Your Own Steep 2 teaspoons crushed or minced dried orange peel (preferably sour) for 2 days in 1 cup sweet, nonsparkling white wine. Strain through a fine-mesh sieve; discard the peel. Use 1 tablespoon for each tablespoon in the recipe. Store in a sterilized jar in the refrigerator; it will keep for up to 7 days.

OYSTER MUSHROOMS/PLEUROTUS/SHIMEJI/HIRATAKE, FRESH – 4 ounces

- 4 ounces fresh eringi, enoki, or straw mushrooms
- 2 to 3 ounces canned oyster, enoki, or straw mushrooms
- 4 ounces fresh shiitake mushroom caps

OYSTER SAUCE (Chinese cooking condiment) – 1 tablespoon

- 1 tablespoon Thai oyster sauce/*nam man hoi* (less salty; more oyster flavor)
- 1 tablespoon vegetarian oyster-flavored sauce or Lee Kum Kee Vegetarian Stir-Fry Sauce (contains mushrooms and vegetable proteins)
- 1 1/2 teaspoons mushroom or dark soy sauce and 1 1/2 teaspoons black bean sauce
- 1 teaspoon Asian fish sauce mixed with 2 teaspoons *kecap manis* or Chinese or Thai sweet black soy sauce
- 1 tablespoon teriyaki sauce (sweeter)
- 1 teaspoon Maggi Seasoning

P

PALM KERNEL OIL (Southeast Asian mild, light colored oil) – 1 cup
- ☞ 1 cup refined melted coconut oil or mild-flavored olive oil

PALM LEAVES (for wrapping and steaming) See WRAPPERS FOR FOOD, NON-EDIBLE

PALM SUGAR, LIGHT/COCONUT PALM SUGAR (Southeast Asian unrefined sugar) –1 (1-inch) piece chopped or shaved See also JAGGERY
- ☞ 2 tablespoons coconut sugar crystals or Sucanat
- ☞ 1 tablespoon each maple sugar and light brown sugar
- ☞ 2 tablespoons firmly packed light brown sugar
- ☞ 4 teaspoons granulated sugar

PALM SUGAR SYRUP, HEAVY – 1 cup
- ☞ 2 cups light palm sugar, melted over very low heat until liquefied (add a little maple syrup if desired)
- ☞ 1 cup each shaved palm sugar and water, simmered until thick and syrupy
- ☞ 1 cup golden syrup, such as Lyle's

PALM SUGAR SYRUP, LIGHT – 1 cup
- ☞ 1 cup each shaved (or jarred) palm sugar and water heated until sugar dissolves
- ☞ 1 cup simple/stock syrup

PALM SYRUP See COCONUT NECTAR

PALM VINEGAR/COCONUT PALM VINEGAR/SIRKA/SUKA NG NIYOG (Indian, Filipino, and Southeast Asian) – 1 tablespoon
- ☞ 1 tablespoon unseasoned mild rice vinegar, such as Japanese

☞ 2 teaspoons champagne vinegar, coconut vinegar, or white wine vinegar and 1 teaspoon water
☞ 1 1/2 teaspoons each cider vinegar and water

PANANG CURRY PASTE (Thai seasoning) – 1 tablespoon
☞ 1 tablespoon red curry paste (stronger-tasting)

PANDAN LEAF EXTRACT/ESSENCE – 1 tablespoon:
Make Your Own Cut 20 fresh mature (or frozen) pandan leaves into small pieces and pulverize in a high-speed blender with 1/2 cup water. Press through a fine sieve, then measure out 1 tablespoon liquid. The extract will keep refrigerated for up to 1 week.

PANDAN LEAVES/PANDANUS/BAI TOEY/LA DUA/DAUN PANDAN (Southeast Asian flavoring and coloring agent) – 1 fresh or frozen leaf *See also KEWRA ESSENCE*
☞ 1/8 teaspoon pandan syrup, powder, or paste
☞ 2 or 3 drops pandan extract

PANDAN/PANDANUS FLOWER ESSENCE *See KEWRA/KEVDA*

PANEER/PANIR (Indian fresh curd cheese) – 4 ounces
☞ 4 ounces pressed farmer cheese or queso fresco
☞ 4 ounces drained extra-firm tofu
☞ 4 ounces halloumi cheese (saltier; reduce the salt in the recipe by 1/2 teaspoon)

PANKO (Japanese-style crisp, light breadcrumbs) – 1 cup
☞ 1 cup crushed crackers, Melba toasts, or low-sodium tortilla chips
☞ 1 1/2 cups thin, crisp, whole-grain crackers processed using the shredding device (to replace whole-wheat panko)

PAPAYA, GREEN/PAWPAW/MALAKAW – 1 pound
☞ 1 pound tart green apples, such as Granny Smith or Bramley's Seedling (Prevent discoloring by soaking in acidulated water immediately after cutting.)

☞ 1 pound chayote or jicama (for cooking; or grated or shredded for salads)

PARATHA (Indian whole-wheat flatbread) – 1
☞ 1 whole-wheat, whole spelt, or multi-grain tortilla

PEANUT DIPPING SAUCE (Southeast Asian condiment) – 2/3 cup
Make Your Own Stir together 1/4 cup peanut butter, 1/4 cup warm water, and 1 tablespoon each soy sauce, seasoned rice vinegar, and Chinese chili-garlic sauce.
Or
Heat 1/3 cup smooth peanut butter, 1/3 cup well-shaken canned coconut milk, and 1 teaspoon Sriracha over low heat, stirring until smooth, about 5 minutes.

PEANUTS/FA-SANG/MUNG-PHALI/MANI – 1 cup:
☞ 1 cup wild jungle peanuts (heirloom nut from the Amazon; does not contain aflatoxin found in American peanuts)
☞ 1 cup cashews

PEANUTS, ROASTED – 1 pound
☞ Spread 1 pound raw shelled peanuts on a baking sheet and bake in a preheated 350° F oven for 10 minutes.

PEA SHOOTS/TENDRILS/DAU MIU/DOU MIAO – 1 cup See also SHOOTS AND SPROUTS
☞ 1 cup chickweed tips/*Stellaria media*
☞ 1 cup watercress or garden cress sprigs, thick stems removed
☞ 1 cup baby arugula or baby spinach, sliced lengthwise
☞ 1 cup shredded or thinly sliced snow peas or snap peas (about 4 ounces)

PEPPERCORNS, CUBEB/TAILED PEPPER (Indonesian seasoning) – 1 tablespoon
☞ 1 tablespoon allspice berries

☞ 2 teaspoons coarsely crushed black peppercorns mixed with a few toasted crushed Szechuan peppercorns

PEPPERCORNS, SICHUAN/SZECHUAN/FAGARA – 1 teaspoon
☞ 1/4 teaspoon sansho powder/*kona-zansho* and 1/4 teaspoon ground black pepper
☞ 1/4 teaspoon crushed dried Tasmanian pepperberries/mountain pepper
☞ 1/2 teaspoon black peppercorns and 1/8 teaspoon finely grated lemon zest

PERILLA *See SHISO, GREEN/PERILLA LEAF*

PINE NUTS/PIGNOLI/PINYON/PIÑON/JAHT – 1 cup shelled
☞ 1 cup sunflower seed kernels, pumpkin seed kernels/*pepitas*, or hempseeds
☞ 1 cup slivered blanched almonds

PISTACHIO NUTS/PISTA – 1 cup dried shelled
☞ 1 cup pine nuts, almonds, or hazelnuts

PIXIAN CHILI BEAN SAUCE *See SICHUAN CHILI BEAN PASTE*

PLUM SAUCE/DUCK SAUCE/TIM CHEON/SU MUI JEONG (Chinese condiment) – 1/2 cup
☞ 1/2 cup mango chutney, thinned with a little vinegar
☞ 1/4 cup apricot or peach jam, 1/4 cup plum jam, 1 tablespoons cider vinegar, and 1/2 teaspoon sugar simmered until slightly thickened, about 5 minutes (the sauce will thicken further as it cools)

PLUM WINE/UMESHU (Japanese) – 1 cup
☞ 1 cup Chinese plum wine/*mui jow*, or sweet sherry, preferably Oloroso

POMEGRANATE SEEDS, DRIED SOUR/ANARDANA (Indian souring agent) – 1 tablespoon

- 1 tablespoon pomegranate molasses, lemon juice, or lime juice (for a souring agent)
- 1 tablespoon snipped dried barberries or cranberries (for garnish)

PONZU SAUCE (Japanese citrus shoyu sauce) – 1/3 cup

Make Your Own Stir together 2 tablespoons each Japanese soy sauce and dashi (or kombu stock) and yuzu juice (or lemon or lime juice), then sweeten to taste with 1 tablespoon mirin (or sugar).

POPPY SEEDS, YELLOW-WHITE/KASHASH/KHUS KHUS (Indian thickening and seasoning agent) – 1 cup:

- 1 cup black amaranth grain softened in hot water 8 to 12 hours
- 1 cup sesame seed, hulled hempseed; light flaxseed, salba seed, or lamb's quarters seed

PORCINI MUSHROOM/KING BOLETE/PENNY BUN/CÈPE, FRESH – 1 pound

- 1 pound fresh portobello mushrooms, gills removed
- 3 ounces dried porcini/*cèpes* or dried Polish mushrooms, soaked in warm water until softened, 30 to 40 minutes
- 3 ounces dried shiitake mushrooms (for more meaty, umami flavor) soaked in warm water until softened, 30 to 40 minutes
- 1 (10-ounce) can whole or quartered *cèpes*

PORCINI POWDER – 1/3 cup See also MUSHROOM POWDER

Make Your Own Break up 1/2 ounce (3 or 4) smooth or cleaned dried porcini mushrooms and grind to a fine powder in a coffee/spice grinder. Sift out large pieces, then regrind and sift again. Store in an airtight container in a cool, dark place; it will keep for up to 3 months.

PORK BELLY, FRESH, 1 pound

- 1 pound unsmoked slab bacon (fresh whole)
- 1 pound fatty pork shoulder

PORK FAT, RENDERED *See LARD, FRESH LEAF*

PORTOBELLOS/MATURE CREMINI MUSHROOMS, FRESH – 1 pound
- 1 pound large fresh cremini, porcini, or matsutake mushrooms
- 3 ounces dried porcini mushrooms, soaked in warm water until softened, 30 to 40 minutes
- 1 (10-ounce) can whole or sliced mushrooms

POT STICKER DIPPING SAUCE *See ASIAN DIPPING SAUCE*

POT STICKER DUMPLING WRAPPERS *See GYOZA WRAPPERS*

POTOLS/PATOLS/POINTED GOURD (Bangladeshi gourd vegetable) – 1 pound
- 1 pound Mexican squash or small zucchini

PUMMELO/POMELO BLOSSOM ESSENCE/KAO PAN (Thai flavoring agent) – 1 teaspoon
- 1 teaspoon lemon extract

PUMMELO/POMELO/SHADDOCK/JABONG (large yellow-green thick-skinned citrus) – 1
- 1 large Oroblanco citrus (a hybrid of pummelo and grapefruit; juicier)
- 2 or 3 mondelos/mandalos (sweeter; more seeds)
- 2 medium pink grapefruits

PUMPKIN LEAF/GREENS/CUCURBITA MAXIMA (Southeast Asian and African vegetable) – 1 pound
- 1 pound amaranth/Chinese spinach, spinach beet, Swiss chard, or New Zealand spinach

PUMPKIN TIPS (Southeast Asian and African vegetable) – 8 (6-inch) tips
- 1 cup fresh peeled pumpkin, cut into 1/2-inch pieces

Q

QUAIL/PARTRIDGE – 1
- 1 small squab, young pheasant, or guinea hen

QUAIL EGGS, HARD BOILED – 4
- 4 jarred or canned water-packed hardboiled quails' eggs
- 1 large hen egg, hardboiled, shelled and quartered (or 2 small ones, halved)

R

RADISH, ASIAN *See DAIKON*

RADISH SPROUTS *See SHOOTS AND SPROUTS*

RAGI/FINGER MILLET/RED MILLET (Shri Lankan flatbread flour) – 1 cup
  ⇨ 1 cup unbleached whole-wheat flour

RAISINS, HIMALAYAN HUNZA – 1 pound
  1 pound seedless golden raisins or dried red barberries

RAITA (Indian condiment) – 9 ounces
  ⇨ 1/3 cup finely chopped fresh mint, or shredded and drained cucumbers, stirred into 1 cup plain yogurt (full fat, lowfat, or nonfat)

RAMBUTAN/HAIRY LYCHEE/MAMON (Southeast Asian small, white-fleshed fruit)
  ⇨ Fresh, canned, or frozen *pulasans*, longans, or lychees

RANGPUR *See LIME, RANGPUR, JUICE; LIME, RANGPUR, ZEST*

RESHAMPATTI CHILI POWDER (Indian seasoning) – 1 teaspoon
  ⇨ 1 teaspoon ground cayenne pepper

RICE BRAN, ROASTED/IRI NUKA (Japanese preserving medium for nuka pickles/nukazuke) – 1 pound
  ⇨ 1 pound wheat bran, toasted (Toast in a dry skillet over low heat, stirring frequently, until toasty-smelling, 10 to 12 minutes. Cool completely.)

RICE BRAN OIL/KOME-NUKA ABURA (Asian cooking oil with a high smoke point) – 1 cup
☞ 1 cup peanut, corn, or canola oil

RICE CAKE – 1
☞ 1/2 cup unsalted popped popcorn

RICE FLOUR, BROWN – 1 cup
☞ 3/4 cup short-grain brown rice, ground until fine in a grain mill, or in small batches in a spice/coffee grinder, then sieved
☞ 1 cup superfine brown rice flour (less grainy)
☞ 1 cup stone-ground garbanzo bean flour, garbanzo–fava bean flour blend such as Authentic Foods Garfava Flour, or Indian *besan*/gram or urad dal flour
☞ 1 cup premade gluten-free flour blend, preferably brown rice–based

RICE FLOUR, CHINESE/ZHAN MI FEN See RICE FLOUR, WHITE, SUPERFINE

RICE FLOUR, SWEET/GLUTINOUS/MOCHIKO/SHIRATAMAJO – 1 tablespoon for thickening
☞ 2 tablespoons short-grain sweet/glutinous white rice, ground in a spice/coffee grinder until powder, then measured
☞ 2 tablespoons tapioca starch; or 5 teaspoons pearl or quick-cooking tapioca, ground in a spice/coffee grinder until powdery, about 30 seconds
☞ 1 tablespoon cornstarch (separates when frozen)
☞ 2 1/4 teaspoons potato starch (separates when frozen)
☞ 4 teaspoons arrowroot powder (separates when frozen)
☞ 3 tablespoons kudzu powder (separates when frozen)
☞ 2 tablespoons all-purpose or quick-mixing flour (cook at least 5 more minutes after thickened; separates when frozen)

RICE FLOUR, WHITE, SUPERFINE – 1 cup
☞ 3/4 cup plus 2 tablespoons long-grain packaged white rice, or dry Cream of Rice cereal, ground until powdery in a high-powered

blender, or in small batches in a spice/coffee grinder. Sift, then re-grind if necessary (slightly coarser)

RICE MALT SWEETENER/RICE SYRUP *See MIZUAME*

RICE MILK POWDER – 1 cup
⇨ 1 cup soy milk powder

RICE PADDY HERB/NGO OM/MA OM/PHAK KHAYANG (Southeast Asian seasoning) – 4 or 5 sprigs (1 tablespoon chopped)
⇨ 5 or 6 fresh cilantro sprigs (for flavor or for garnish)
⇨ 1/4 teaspoon whole cumin seeds, or 1/8 teaspoon ground cumin (for flavor)

RICE PAPER WRAPPERS/BANH UOT, FRESH OR FROZEN (Vietnamese) – 8 ounces
⇨ 8 ounces dried spring roll wrappers/*banh trang*, individually dipped in water to soften
⇨ 8 ounces phyllo dough, cut to size
⇨ 8 ounces paper-thin crepes

RICE POWDER, ROASTED/KAO KUA PON/THINH/TEPUNG BERTIH (Southeast Asian thickening agent) – 1/2 cup
⇨ 1/2 cup uncooked sticky rice toasted in a dry skillet over medium heat, stirring frequently, until golden, 8 to 10 minutes; cooled, then ground in small batches in a spice/coffee grinder until sandy-textured; store, tightly covered, in the refrigerator (for best flavor store toasted rice and grind just before using). For Chinese brown rice powder/*chau mi fen*, use brown rice
⇨ 1/2 cup toasted chickpea/garbanzo flour

RICE STARCH, GLUTINOUS *See RICE FLOUR, SWEET/GLUTINOUS*

RICE SYRUP *See BROWN RICE SYRUP*

RICE VINEGAR – 1 tablespoon See also JAPANESE RICE VINEGAR; KOREAN BROWN RICE VINEGAR

- 1 tablespoon champagne vinegar, cava vinegar, or white wine vinegar
- 2 teaspoons cider vinegar or distilled white vinegar, 1 teaspoon water, and 2 or 3 grains sugar

RICE WINE See CHINESE YELLOW RICE COOKING WINE; JAPANESE RICE WINE; KOREAN RICE WINE; MIRIN; SAKÉ; SHAOXING

RICE, BASMATI AGED WHITE (Indian long-grain fragrant Dehra Dun/ Dehraduni rice)

- 1 cup Kohinoor, Pari, or Tilda basmati rice
- 1 cup domestic basmati-type rice, such as Calmati, Jasmati, Kasmati, Mahatma, or Texmati (shorter grain; stickier)
- 1 cup baby basmati rice/*Kalijira* (fragrant; known as king of rice)
- 1 cup long-grain brown basmati rice (crunchier texture; double the water and cooking time; or reduce the cooking time by soaking the rice for 6 to 10 hours)
- 1 cup white Thai jasmine rice (smaller grain; stickier texture)
- 1 cup Patna long-grain Indian rice (less fragrant)
- 1 1/3 cups domestic parboiled rice, such as Uncle Ben's converted rice

RICE, BHUTANESE RED (partially milled, medium-grain chewy texture) – 1 cup

- 1 cup French Camargue red rice
- 1 cup California Calusari red rice
- 1 cup Wehani rice
- 1 cup long- or medium-grain brown rice

RICE, BROWN JASMINE – 1 cup

- 1 cup brown basmati rice, brown Texmati rice, Wehani rice, or wild pecan rice

RICE, BROWN, QUICK-COOKING – 1 1/2 cups uncooked
- ☞ 1 cup plus 2 tablespoons short-grain, regular brown rice soaked in water for at least 4 hours, then drained and cooked in 2 1/2 cups fresh water for 20 minutes
- ☞ 1 cup long-grain, regular brown rice cooked in 2 to 3 quarts boiling water for 22 to 25 minutes (firmer and fluffier)
- ☞ 1 cup long-grain regular brown rice, washed, drained, then cooked with 1 1/4 cups fresh water in a pressure cooker for 20 minutes

RICE, BURMESE See RICE, THAI JASMINE WHITE

RICE, CHINESE BLACK, STICKY/FORBIDDEN (medium-grain unmilled) – 1 cup
- ☞ 1 cup Thai long-grain, black/purple sticky rice
- ☞ 1 cup white sweet/glutinous rice (lacks color)
- ☞ 1 cup Italian long-grain black rice, such as *riso venere* (for the color only)
- ☞ 1 cup black barley (chewier)

RICE, CHINESE-TYPE WHITE/FAN – 1 cup
- ☞ 1 cup long- or medium-grain white rice (cook without salt)
- ☞ 1 cup jasmine rice (cook without salt)

RICE, FILIPINO BLACK/PIRURU TONG See RICE, CHINESE BLACK/ FORBIDDEN

RICE, HIMALAYAN RED – 1 cup
- ☞ 1 cup Wehani rice
- ☞ 1/2 cup each long-grain brown rice and wild rice

RICE, INDIAN/PAKISTANI LONG-GRAIN See RICE, BASMATI AGED WHITE

RICE, INDONESIAN LONG-GRAIN (Cianjur) See RICE, THAI JASMINE

RICE, JAPANESE SHORT- GRAIN JAPONICA/URUCHIMAE (such as Aki-takomachi, Hitomebore, Sasanisiki, or Tamanishiki) – 1 cup

- 1 cup California-grown Japanese-style rice, such as Calrose Asia, Kagayaki, Kahomai, Kokhuto, Koshihikari, Lundberg Sushi, Maruyu, Matsu, Minori, Nishiki, or Shiragiju
- 1 cup short-grain rice, such as Arborio, Blue rose, or Calrose
- 1 cup semi-milled Japanese haiga rice/*haigamai* (white rice with the rice germ; cross between white and brown rice)
- 1 cup Japanese-style short-grain brown rice/*genmai* (longer cooking time)

RICE, JAPANESE SWEET, GLUTINOUS WHITE/MOCHIGOME See RICE, STICKY/SWEET/GLUTINOUS

RICE, JASMINE FRAGRANT See RICE, THAI JASMINE WHITE

RICE, KOREAN/BAKMI (short-grain white rice) – 1 cup

- 1 cup short- or medium-grain white rice, such as Chung-Jeon, Blue rose, Calrose, or Calriso
- 1 cup short-grain brown rice/*hyunmi* or Japanese-style brown rice, such as Lundberg's (longer cooking time)

RICE, KOREAN SWEET/GLUTINOUS WHITE/CHAPSSALGARU See RICE, STICKY/SWEET/GLUTINOUS

RICE, PUFFED BASMATI/KURMURA (Indian) – 1 cup

- 1 cup puffed rice cereal, puffed wheat, or air-puffed millet or sorghum

RICE, RED (semi-milled, whole-grain) – 1 cup

- 1 cup Bhutanese red medium-grain, Camargue red medium- to short-grain, Himalayan red long-grain, Thai red long-grain or short-grain cargo, or Vietnamese red medium-grain cargo
- 1 cup domestic short-grain Christmas rice
- 1 cup domestic medium-grain Calusari or long-grain Wehani

RICE, STICKY/SWEET/GLUTINOUS – 1 cup

- ☞ 1 cup West Bengali short-grain white sticky rice/*gobindavog*
- ☞ 1 cup Botan rice
- ☞ 1 cup brown sweet/glutinous rice
- ☞ 1 cup Thai black/purple sticky rice or Chinese black/forbidden rice (less sticky)

RICE, SUSHI See RICE, JAPANESE SHORT-GRAIN JAPONICA

RICE, THAI JASMINE RED/PURPLE/KHAO HOM MALI (unmilled long-grain) – 1 cup

- ☞ 1/2 cup each Thai black sticky rice and white jasmine rice cooked together

RICE, THAI JASMINE WHITE/KHAO HOM MALI (aromatic long-grain) – 1 cup

- ☞ 1 cup domestic jasmine rice, such as Mahatma or Texmati
- ☞ 1/2 cup brown jasmine rice (chewier texture; increase the cooking time)
- ☞ 1 cup Indian basmati or Patna rice (less moist; lacks aroma)
- ☞ 1 cup basmati or long-grain white rice, cooked in jasmine-scented water (Steep 1 or 2 jasmine tea bags, 1 1/2 tablespoons jasmine-tea pearls, or 1 unsprayed jasmine flower in 2 cups boiling water for 5 minutes; remove the tea bags, pearls, or flower and use the water as the cooking liquid for the rice.)
- ☞ 1 cup broken jasmine rice (less expensive)

RICE, THAI STICKY BLACK/KHAO NIAO DAHM (unmilled, long-grain; chewy when cooked) – 1 cup

- ☞ 1 cup Chinese black rice/forbidden rice
- ☞ 1 cup Thai sweet/glutinouss white rice (stickier; lacks color)

RICE, THAI STICKY WHITE/KHAO NIAO (long-grain; sticky when cooked) – 1 cup

- ☞ 1 cup short- or medium-grain Chinese or Japanese sweet/glutinous rice

☞ 1 cup domestic sticky white rice, such as Lundberg's
☞ 1 cup Thai sticky unmilled black rice (less sticky, chewier; takes longer to cook)

ROASTED BARLEY TEA/MUGICHA/BORICHA See KOREAN ROASTED BARLEY TEA/BORICHA

ROCK SUGAR See SUGAR, BROWN ROCK; SUGAR, YELLOW/CLEAR ROCK

ROSE PETALS, WILD FRESH/DOK GULAB (Southeast Asian aromatic garnish) – 1 cup
☞ 1 cup fresh, pesticide-free Rugosa or pink damask rose petals (cut off the white part at the base of each petal; it is bitter)
☞ 1 cup fresh, pesticide-free nasturtium petals, or other colorful petals
See FLOWERS/BLOSSOMS/PETALS, FRESH EDIBLE

ROSE WATER/GULAAB JAL (food flavoring agent) – 1 tablespoon
☞ 1 or 2 drops food-grade pure rose extract/essence (reduce the liquid in the recipe by 1 tablespoon)
Make Your Own Simmer 3/4 cup purified water and 1/2 cup trimmed, fresh, pesticide-free rose petals, covered, for 30 minutes. Cool, strain, then add 1 or 2 teaspoons vodka. Store in a sterilized bottle in the refrigerator. Makes 1/3 cup; use 1 tablespoon for each tablespoon in the recipe. Use within 7 days.

ROTI (Indian whole-wheat flatbread) – 1
☞ 1 chapati, paratha, naan, or whole-wheat pita

ROTI FOUR (Indian whole-wheat flour) – 1 cup
☞ 1/2 cup each whole-wheat flour and all-purpose flour

ROYAL FERN/ZENMAI See FIDDLEHEAD FERNS

ROYAL TRUMPET MUSHROOM See KING OYSTER/ROYAL TRUMPET MUSHROOM

S

SAEUJOT/SAEWOO-JEOT *See KOREAN SHRIMP, SALTED/FERMENTED MINI*

SAFFRON/COUPÉ/SARGOL/KESAR – 1/2 teaspoon (10 to 15 threads/ pinch):
- 1/8 teaspoon ground/powdered saffron
- 2 or 3 drops of saffron extract
- 1 1/2 teaspoons safflower stigmas/Mexican saffron/*azafrán* soaked in 1 tablespoon warm water 20 minutes, then added to the dish along with the water (for color)
- 1 teaspoon pesticide-free dried marigold petals, preferably pot marigold/*Calendula officinalis*, steeped in 1 or 2 tablespoon warm water 5 minutes; use liquid for color and discard petals
- 1/2 teaspoon ground annatto seeds (for color)
- 1 teaspoon whole annatto seeds steeped in a little hot liquid; use liquid for color and discard seeds (for color)
- 1/4 to 1/2 teaspoon powdered Madras turmeric, or just enough for color

SAGO PEARLS/BOT BANG/SABUDANA/SAGUDANA – 1 tablespoon
- 1 tablespoon tapioca pearls, 1/8-inch diameter or smaller (slightly starchier)

SAGO STARCH – 1 tablespoon
- 1 tablespoon tapioca starch, or 2 1/2 teaspoons quick-cooking tapioca, ground until powdery
- 2 teaspoons arrowroot powder
- 1 1/2 teaspoons cornstarch or sweet/glutinous rice flour
- 2 tablespoons all-purpose flour or quick-mixing flour, such as Wondra (cook 5 minutes after thickening)

SAKÉ/JAPANESE RICE WINE/FUTSU-SHU – 1/4 cup for cooking
- 2 to 3 tablespoons sake-based mirin, such as *aji no haha* or *aske mirin*; reduce the sugar in the recipe accordingly
- 1/4 cup Chinese yellow rice wine/Shaoxing
- 1/4 cup dry sherry, such as Dry Sack, or dry vermouth
- 1/4 cup white wine plus a pinch of brown sugar

SALAM LEAF/INDONESIAN BAY LEAF/DAUN SALAM/ (Indian seasoning) – 1 (3-inch) dried leaf
- 2 or 3 fresh curry leaves plus a few drops of lime juice

SALMON ROE See *IKURA*

SALMON, SALTED, FLAKES/SHIO ZAKE (Japanese) – 1 pound
- 1 pound poached salmon, flaked and lightly sprinkled with salt

SALT, BLACK/KALA NAMAK (unrefined Indian salt) – 1 tablespoon
- 1 tablespoon Hawaiian coarse-grain black lava sea salt (slightly smoky flavor)
- 1 tablespoon Cyprus medium-grain black lava sea salt flakes (for finishing)
- 4 teaspoons table salt or sea salt (for cooking; lacks sulphuric aroma and flavor)

SAMBAL MANIS (Indonesian dipping sauce) – 1 tablespoon
- 1 tablespoon sambal oelek (hotter)

SAMBAL OELEK (Indonesian hot chili paste) – 1 tablespoon
- 3 stemmed fresh bird's eye chilis (or other small red chilis), simmered in 1/4 cup vinegar for 5 minutes; drained, cooled, and crushed to a coarse paste with a pinch each of salt and brown sugar (Wear plastic gloves when handling the chilis and avoid touching your face.)
- 1 (or more) tablespoons Indonesian dipping sauce/*sambal manis* (milder)

- ☞ 1 tablespoon harissa, Sriracha, Vietnamese chili sauce/*tuong ot toi*, Chinese hot chili paste/*la jiao jiang*, or Japanese chili yuzu paste/*yuzu koshu*
- ☞ 2 teaspoons chopped Thai chilis
- ☞ 1 to 2 teaspoon hot pepper sauce, such as Tabasco, or hot chili powder, such as cayenne

SAMOSA DOUGH (Indian) – 8 ounces
- ☞ 8 ounces egg roll wrappers, Shanghai spring roll skins, or lumpia wrappers, cut to size (for frying)
- ☞ 8 ounces frozen mini phyllo shells, or phyllo pastry sheets cut to size (for baking)

SANAAM CHILIS/LONG CHILIS, DRIED (Indian) – 3 or 4
- ☞ 3 or 4 dried de árbol, cayenne, or Thai red chilis
- ☞ 1/3 to 1/2 teaspoon ground cayenne pepper or Thai chili powder

SAND GINGER See GALANGAL, LESSER

SANSHO LEAVES/PRICKLY ASH LEAVES/KINOME, FRESH See KINOME

SANSHO POWDER/PRICKLY ASH POWDER/KONA-ZANSHO/SANSYO (Japanese seasoning) – 1 teaspoon
- ☞ 1 teaspoon lemon pepper seasoning; reduce the salt and pepper in the recipe accordingly

SATAW/SATOR BEAN/BITTER BEAN/PETAI (Southeast Asian) – 1 cup
- ☞ 1 cup young fresh shelled and peeled fava beans
- ☞ 1 cup thawed frozen lima beans, peeled
- ☞ 1 cup fresh or frozen snap or snow peas

SATAY SAUCE See PEANUT DIPPING SAUCE

SAWLEAF/SAWTOOTH HERB See CULANTRO

SCALLION OIL/MO HAHN (Vietnamese seasoning oil) – 1/2 cup:
Make Your Own Cook 1/2 cup thinly sliced scallions (green part only) in 1/2 cup vegetable oil until they wilt and change color, about 10 seconds. Let the mixture cool, then strain. The oil will keep, refrigerated, for up to 2 weeks.

SCALLIONS/GREEN ONIONS – 4 ounces
- 4 ounces spring onions, Egyptian onions, Mexican onions, ramp bulbs, onion sprouts, young thin leeks, garlic shoots, or young shallot tops

SCREWPINE LEAF See PANDAN LEAVES

SEAWEED See ARAME; HIJIKI; KOMBU; MOZUKU; NORI; WAKAME

SEAWEED SEASONING/GARNISH – 1 tablespoon
- 1 tablespoon shredded nori with sesame seeds/*nori komi furikake*
- 1 tablespoon crushed wakame or nori (sheets toasted, then coarsely crushed; or pretoasted nori sheets/*yaki-nori* coarsely crushed)
- 1 tablespoon crumbled seasoned nori strips/*ajitsuke-nori*
- 1 to 2 teaspoons powdered nori/*ao nori/aosa*, or powered sea lettuce/green laver powder

SESAME CHILI OIL See CHILI OIL, CHINESE

SESAME LEAF See SHISO, GREEN

SESAME OIL, TOASTED/GOMA ABURA/MA YAU/DAU ME/XIANG YOU (Asian seasoning) – 1 tablespoon
- 1 teaspoon peanut oil mixed with 2 teaspoons ground toasted sesame seeds (or untoasted seeds dry-toasted, then ground)
- 1 tablespoon Indian sesame oil/*gingelly/til ka tel*
- 1 tablespoon roasted peanut oil

SESAME PASTE/GOMA PASTE/ZHI MA JIANG/NERI-GOMA (Chinese and Japanese seasoning) – 1 tablespoon

- 1 tablespoon tahini plus few drops toasted sesame oil
- 1 tablespoon smooth unsweetened peanut butter plus few drops light/untoasted sesame oil

Make Your Own Toast 1 tablespoon white unhulled sesame seeds in a dry skillet over medium heat, stirring constantly, until golden, 1 to 2 minutes; then grind it in a spice mill/coffee grinder, with 1 teaspoon sesame oil (or soy oil) and a pinch of salt until reduced to a paste.

SESAME SALT/GOMASHIO (Japanese condiment) – 1/3 cup (about)

- 1/3 cup packaged smoked sesame seeds/*shirogoma*

Make Your Own Toast 1/2 cup black sesame seeds in a dry skillet over medium heat, stirring constantly, until fragrant, 3 to 4 minutes (or in a preheated 350°F oven for 5 to 7 minutes). Cool, then coarsely grind it in a spice mill/coffee grinder with 1 tablespoon coarse sea salt (or kosher salt). For 1 teaspoon, grind 1 teaspoon toasted sesame seeds plus few grains of sea salt in a salt mill or mortar.

SESAME SEEDS, BLACK OR WHITE/MUKI GOMA/TIL (Japanese and Indian condiment) – 1 ounce

- 1 ounce white poppy seeds, sunflower seed kernels, golden flaxseeds, hulled hemp seeds, salba seeds, or finely chopped blanched almonds

SHALLOTS, ASIAN/HOM DAENG/BAWANG MERAH/BRAMBANG, FRESH (small, purplish clove) – 1 bunch/3 or 4 small

- 2 red pearl onions, halved lengthwise
- 1 medium shallot
- 1 very small red onion

SHALLOTS, CHINESE/TON HORM – 3 to 4 small, or 2 medium, or 1 extra-large

- 1 bunch scallions or spring onions

- 2 to 3 tablespoons freeze-dried shallots, softened in 2 tablespoons warm water for 10 minutes
- 6 Asian purple shallots (smaller, milder, and less moist) or Egyptian walking onions

SHALLOTS, FRIED, PACKAGED/CHIÊN HAHN HUONG (Vietnamese garnish) – 1 cup

- 1 cup (2 ounces) packaged fried onions, such as Indonesian *bawang goreng*
- 1 cup (2 ounces) canned domestic fried onions, such as French's

Make Your Own Thinly slice 5 or 6 shallots, then fry in 1/3 cup hot oil until crisp and golden, about 4 minutes. Drain on paper towels. (For a more pronounced flavor, add the shallots to cold oil and cook on medium heat until golden.)

SHANGHAI BOK CHOY/BOK CHOY SHOOTS – 1 pound

- 1 pound baby bok choy/*li ren choi*, or regular bok choy cut into 3-inch pieces

SHANGHAI NOODLES, FRESH – 1 pound

- 12 ounces dried bucatini, perciatelli, spaghetti grossi, or other thick, oval, white wheat noodles

SHAOXING/SHAO HSING/HUANG JUI (Chinese yellow rice wine, 36% proof) – 1 cup

- 1 cup Shaoxing cooking wine/*liao jiu/chiew* (contains salt)
- 1 cup glutinous yellow rice wine/*gnow mei dew*
- 1 cup medium-dry sherry, such as amontillado
- 1 cup dry vermouth

SHEMIJI/SHIMIJI MUSHROOM *See OYSTER MUSHROOM*

SHICHIMI TOGARASHI *See JAPANESE SEVEN-SPICE SEASONING*

SHIITAKE MUSHROOMS/PYOGO, FRESH – 1 pound

☞ 3 ounces dried shiitake mushrooms, soaked in hot water for 30 minutes, stem sides down and weighted with a saucer, squeezed dry, and stems discarded (The strained soaking water can be reserved for another use. For more deeply flavored mushrooms, soak for 8 to 12 hours in cool water.)

☞ 3 ounces dried flower mushrooms/*hua gu/hana/donko* (thick variety of shiitake with a more potent flavor; soak for 1 hour in hot water)

☞ 1 pound fresh cremini or matsutake mushrooms

SHIITAKE POWDER – 1/3 cup (packed)

☞ 1/2 ounce dried shiitake mushrooms, cleaned and ground in a spice/coffee grinder or blender until fine

☞ 1/3 cup porcini powder

SHINSHU MISO *See MISO, LIGHT/SHIRO/SHINSHU/SAIKYO*

SHISHITO PEPPER/SHISHITO-TOGARASHI, FRESH (Japanese small green pepper) – 3 or 4

☞ 3 or 4 Japanese green fushimi peppers/*fushimi-togarashi*

☞ 3 or 4 Spanish Padrón peppers

☞ 1 green Cubanelle pepper, or Italian frying pepper, cut into 1-inch-wide strips

☞ 1 medium green bell pepper or Anaheim chili, peeled and cut into 1-inch-wide strips

SHISO, GREEN/PERILLA LEAF/OHBO/AOJISO/GAENIP/TULKKAE/LA TIA TO, FRESH (Japanese seasoning and garnish) – 1 leaf

☞ 1 to 2 fresh wild shiso leaves/*Perilla frutescens* (smaller leaves; more flavorful)

☞ 1 fresh Vietnamese green/purple perilla/*la tia to* (stronger flavor; less expensive)

☞ 3 fresh holy basil, Thai basil, lemon basil, or anise basil leaves

- 2 fresh sweet basil leaves (Italian, French, or California) and 2 mint leaves
- 2 to 3 watercress or mint sprigs, baby spinach, baby arugula, or other small fresh leaves (for salad or garnish)s
- 1 flat-leaf spinach leaf or palm-size lettuce leaf (for wrapping and shiso rolls)

SHISO, RED/PERILLA LEAF/BEEFSTEAK PLANT/AKAJISO/SHISO ZOJ, FRESH – 1 leaf

- 2 or 3 purple basil leaves, such as Dark Opal, Red Rubin, Purple Delight, or Purple Ruffles added just before cooking ends, or for garnish (loses color when cooked)
- 1 dried red shiso leaf, or a generous pinch of shiso powder (for coloring)

SHOOTS AND SPROUTS (tender new growth of germinated seeds) – 1 ounce

- 1 ounce adzuki/aduki (slightly sweet), alfalfa (mild), amaranth (mild), arugula (peppery), barley (starchy and mild), broccoli (mild), buckwheat (starchy and hearty), cabbage (mild), chickpea (mild), chive (peppery), clover (mild), daikon (peppery), fenugreek (slightly bitter), kale (mild), kamut (mild), leek (peppery), lentil (mild), millet (mild), mitsuba (peppery), mustard (peppery), mung bean (nutty and crunchy), onion (peppery), pumpkin (nutty and crunchy), quinoa (mild), radish (peppery), red clover (mild), soybean (nutty and crunchy), or sunflower (nutty and crunchy)
- 1 ounce snow peas, cut into narrow strips
- 1 ounce pea shoots, tender chickweed tips/*Stellaria media*, or other plant shoots/microgreens

SHRIMP, DRIED/HAY BEE/HAR MAI/HUNG HAENG/TOM KHO (cooking condiment) – 1/4 cup

- 1/4 cup dried crayfish or scallops
- 1/4 cup smoked salted fish, chopped or flaked
- 1 tablespoon minced anchovies, dried salted anchovies, or anchovy paste

- 2 teaspoons pounded (or finely chopped) preroasted dried shrimp paste
- 1 scant tablespoon fermented fish or fish paste, such as pickled gouramy fish (more pungent)
- 1 tablespoon anchovy paste or 1 1/2 rinsed and mashed salt-packed anchovy fillets
- 1 tablespoon Chinese fermented black beans/*dow see,* Burmese fermented soybean paste/*tua nao,* or Japanese dark miso, such as *inaka* or *hatcho*
- 1 teaspoon Worcestershire sauce plus 1/2 teaspoon red miso/*inaka miso*

SHRIMP PASTE, FERMENTED/BAGOONG/BLACHAN/KAPI/MAM TOM/NGAPI/TRASI/XIA JIANG (Southeast Asian pungent seasoning) – 1/2-inch cube

- 2 teaspoons pounded (or finely chopped) preroasted dried shrimp paste
- 1 scant tablespoon fermented fish or fish paste, such as pickled gouramy fish (more pungent)
- 1 tablespoon anchovy paste or 1 1/2 rinsed and mashed salt-packed anchovy fillets
- 1 tablespoon Chinese fermented black beans/*dow see,* Burmese fermented soybean paste/*tua nao,* or Japanese dark miso, such as *inaka* or *hatcho*
- 1 teaspoon Worcestershire sauce plus 1/2 teaspoon red miso/*inaka miso*

SHRIMP POWDER, DRIED/SHRIMP FLOSS/PAZUN CHAUK (Asian flavoring and thickener) – 1/2 cup (packed)

- 1/2 cup toasted chickpea flour plus 1 or 2 teaspoons dark Japanese miso, such as *hatcho,* or Burmese fermented soybean paste/*tuo nao* (for vegan option)

Make Your Own Toast a scant 1/2 cup dried shrimp in a dry skillet over low heat for 4 to 5 minutes, then grind to a fine powder in a blender or spice/coffee grinder. Store, tightly sealed, in the freezer. Alternatively, soak the shrimp to cover until softened, 20 to 30 minutes; pat dry, then pulse in a food processor until flossy.

SHRIMP SAUCE, FERMENTED/HOM HA/HAE KOH/BALICHAO/MAM RUOC/PETIS (Southeast Asian jarred seasoning) – 1 tablespoon

- ☞ 1 tablespoon Chinese jarred fermented shrimp/*xia jiang*
- ☞ 2 tablespoons fish sauce, such as *nam pla, nuoc nam, patis* or *shottsuru,* plus a dash of oyster sauce
- ☞ 1 tablespoon anchovy paste, anchovy essence/syrup, or 1 1/2 rinsed and mashed salted anchovy fillets, thinned with a little soy sauce

SHRIMP STOCK – 1 cup

- ☞ 1 cup quick shrimp stock (Put 1 to 2 cups rinsed shrimp shells and heads in a small saucepan and barely cover with cold water; bring to a gentle boil, and simmer, covered, for 10 to 15 minutes; strain. Alternatively, heat the shells and heads in a dry pan until they turn pink before adding the water.)
- ☞ 1/2 to 1 teaspoon shrimp-flavored bouillon powder dissolved in 1 cup hot water

SHUNGIKU See CHRYSANTHEMUM LEAVES, EDIBLE

SICHUAN CHILI BEAN PASTE/PIXIAN CHILI BEAN SAUCE/ DOUBANJIANG/TOBAN JHAN (Chinese condiment) – 1/3 cup

- ☞ 1/4 cup fermented black beans/*douchi*, rinsed briefly in a fine sieve, then mashed with 1 1/2 tablespoons Chinese chili sauce or chili-garlic sauce
- ☞ 1/3 cup Korean chili bean paste/*gochujang*

SICHUAN PEPPER/ANISE PEPPER/DRIED PRICKLY ASH/SANSHO/HUĀ JIĀO (Chinese seasoning) – 1 teaspoon ground/powdered

- ☞ 1/4 teaspoon each ground anise and allspice
- ☞ 1 or 2 teaspoons Sichuan pepper salt/*hu jiao yeni*; reduce salt in the recipe accordingly

▷ 1/2 teaspoon Chinese five-spice powder (only if it contains ground Sichuan peppercorns, not regular peppercorns)

Make Your Own Toast 1 tablespoon Sichuan peppercorns in a dry skillet over low heat until very fragrant and slightly darkened, 4 to 5 minutes. Crush with a mortar or rolling pin while hot, then sift through a fine-mesh sieve and measure (or cool, grind, sift, and measure). Discard the husks.

SICHUAN PEPPER OIL/HUĀ JIĀO YOU (Chinese seasoning) – 2/3 cup

Make Your Own Heat 1/4 cup toasted Sichuan peppercorns and 1 cup peanut oil over low heat for 10 minutes. Cool, then strain into a sterilized jar or bottle. Store, tightly covered, in the refrigerator. It will keep up to 6 months. (Toast the peppercorns in a dry skillet over low heat until fragrant, 4 to 5 minutes.)

SICHUAN PEPPERCORNS/FAGARA See PEPPERCORNS, SICHUAN/ SZECHUAN/FAGARA

SICHUAN RED CHILI OIL/HONG YOU (chili and spice-infused oil) – 1 teaspoon

▷ 1 teaspoon Chinese savory chili oil/*chiu chow*
▷ 1 teaspoon Japanese chili oil/*rayu*

SICHUAN SALT/HUĀ JIĀO YAN (Chinese condiment) – 1/4 cup (about)

Make Your Own Toast 1 tablespoon Sichuan peppercorns and 3 tablespoons coarse sea salt in a dry skillet over low heat until the pepper starts to smoke faintly and the salt is slightly colored, about 5 minutes. Cool, sift, and grind to a powder. (For a coarser texture, toast and grind the peppercorns, then add to the untoasted salt.)

SICHUAN SWEET BEAN PASTE/SAUCE/TIAN MIAN JIANG/TENMENJAN (Chinese condiment) – 1 tablespoon

▷ 2 teaspoons Chinese cooking sauce (*chee hou* sauce or hoisin) and 1 teaspoon rice vinegar

SINGODA FOUR (Indian thickening agent) – 1 cup
- 1 cup water chestnut starch/powder

SNOW PEA SHOOTS See PEA SHOOTS/TENDRILS/DAU MIAU

SNOW PEAS/CHINESE SNOW PEAS – 1 pound
- 1 pound sugar snap peas, strings removed
- 1 pound Chinese yard-long beans, young green Romano beans, or Spanish Musica beans, trimmed, and cut into segments diagonally (longer cooking time)
- 1 pound broccoli stalks, peeled and thinly sliced (longer cooking time)
- 1 pound young radish seed pods (from radishes gone to seed or from a podding variety, such as Rat's Tail)

SOBA NOODLES See JAPANESE NOODLES, BUCKWHEAT

SOBA SAUCE/KAESHI – 1 scant cup
- 3/4 cup Japanese soy sauce, and 2 tablespoons each mirin and granulated sugar brought to a boil and simmered until sugar dissolves, 2 to 3 minutes; it will keep up to 3 months refrigerated

SOJU See KOREAN RICE LIQUOR

SOOJI/SUJI/RAWA (Indian course-textured semolina flour) – 1 cup
- 1 cup wheat farina or regular dry Cream of Wheat

SORAMAME (Japanese fava/broad beans) – 1 pound
- 1 cup fresh or thawed frozen lima beans
- 1 cup fresh or frozen snap or snow peas

SORGHUM/KAFFIR CORN/JOWAR (Indian cereal grain) – 1 cup
- 1 cup hulled millet (tastes best when lightly toasted in a dry skillet before cooking)

SOUR PLUM/PRUNE/ALOO BUKHARA (Central Asian souring agent) – 1 sour plum
- 1 umeboshi (Japanese salt-pickled dried plum) or 3 *umeboshi-sa* (tiny plum paste balls)
- 2 teaspoons jarred umeboshi puree/sour plum paste/*bainiku/neri-ume,* or pomegranate molasses
- 1 regular prune, soaked in white vinegar or umeboshi plum vinegar for 8 to 10 hours

SOURSOP/GUANÁBANA (large tropical fruit) – 1 pound
- 12 ounces frozen soursop pulp
- 1 pound atemoya, cherimoya, or sweetsop (smaller and sweeter)
- 8 ounces canned soursop nectar/*jugo de guanábana* (for flavor only)

SOY BEANS, YELLOW /SOYABEANS/BHATMAS– 1 cup:
- 1 cup soy splits (for faster cooking)

SOY BUTTER – 2 cups
Make Your Own Combine 3/4 cup powdered soy milk, 3/4 cup water, 1 teaspoon salt in a double boiler and cook for 25 minutes; gradually whisk in 1 cup canola oil and beat until thick. Store, refrigerated, in a tightly sealed container. It will keep for up to 1 month.

SOY MILK – 2 cups
- 1/2 cup soy powder (powdered soy milk) and 1 3/4 cups water, blended until smooth
- 8 ounces soft silken tofu and 1 cup cold water blended until smooth (For thinner soy milk, increase the amount of water; for sweeter soy milk, add 2 teaspoons rice syrup or light agave syrup.)

SOY SAUCE (ALL PURPOSE) – 1 tablespoon
- 1 tablespoon reduced-sodium/lower sodium or lite soy sauce (regular or gluten-free)

- 2 teaspoons tamari soy sauce (contains wheat but naturally brewed and without additives)
- 2 teaspoons gluten-free tamari, such as San-J, Crystal, or Westbrae
- 1 tablespoon citrus-seasoned soy sauce, such as Japanese ponzu-seasoned/*ponzu shoyu* or Filipino calamansi-seasoned/*toyo mansi* (for condiments and dressings)
- 1 tablespoon gluten-free liquid aminos, such as Dr. Bronner's or Bragg's
- 1 tablespoon gluten-free and soy-free coconut aminos, such as Coconut Secret, plus a pinch of salt
- 2 to 3 teaspoons Japanese fermented rice/*shio-koji* or miso (thicker consistency; for cooking)
- 1 tablespoon Maggi Seasoning or oyster sauce (for a small amount)
- 2 teaspoons molasses, 1 teaspoon balsamic vinegar, and a few grains of sugar (for a small amount)
- 1 tablespoon Chinese soy sauce powder/*funmatsu* (for cooking or barbecue dry rubs)

SOY SAUCE, CHINESE DARK/BLACK/TABLE SOY/CHO YO/SEE YAU/LAO CHOU – 1 tablespoon

- 1 tablespoon Japanese organic tamari (wheat-free, naturally fermented, darker, thicker, more flavorful)
- 1 tablespoon Japanese dark soy sauce (darker, slightly sweeter, less salty)
- 1 tablespoon mushroom soy sauce (richer tasting)
- 2 teaspoons Chinese light soy sauce and 1 teaspoon black/dark/sweet soy sauce (Chinese or Thai)
- 1 tablespoon Chinese light soy sauce plus 1/4 teaspoon molasses

SOY SAUCE, CHINESE DOUBLE DARK/DOUBLE BLACK/SWEET/YEWN SHE JIANG (such as Koon Chun) – 1 tablespoon

- 1 tablespoon Malaysian sweet, dark soy sauce/*tim cheong*
- 2 teaspoons Chinese dark soy sauce plus 1 teaspoon brown sugar or molasses

SOY SAUCE, CHINESE LIGHT/PALE OR THIN/JIANG JING/JIANG YAO/ SHENG CHOU – 1 tablespoon

- 1 tablespoon Japanese all-purpose soy sauce/*shoyu*, such as Kikkoman; or Korean soy sauce/*ganjang* (darker, less salty, and a touch sweeter)
- 1 tablespoon Chinese white soy sauce/*yin bai jiang,* or Japanese white soy sauce/*shirojoyu* (a little sweeter, but will not add color)
- 1 tablespoon Chinese dark soy sauce/*cho yo* (thicker, stronger, a little sweeter, and less salty)

SOY SAUCE, FILIPINO CITRUS/TOYOMANSI – 1/3 cup:

- 3 tablespoons soy sauce and 2 tablespoon kalamansi juice

SOY SAUCE, JAPANESE ALL-PURPOSE REGULAR DARK/KOIKUCHI SHOYU (such as Kikkoman) – 1 tablespoon

- 1 tablespoon Japanese organic whole soybean soy sauce/*marudaizu shoyu*, or unpasteurized/raw soy sauce/*nama shoyu* (contains wheat)
- 1 tablespoon Japanese low-salt/reduced-salt soy sauce/*gen'en shoyu* (contains additives)
- 2 1/2 teaspoons Japanese light-colored soy sauce/*usukuchi shoyu* or Chinese regular/light soy sauce (thinner and saltier)
- 1 tablespoon Japanese white soy sauce/*shiro shoyu* (very light colored, mellow, and fairly sweet)
- 1 tablespoon Japanese strong-flavored rich soy sauce/*saishikomi* (dark brown and thick; for sashimi and sushi)

SOY SAUCE, JAPANESE LIGHT-COLORED/USUKUCHI SHOYU (saltier and thinner than all-purpose regular dark soy sauce) – 1 tablespoon

- 1 tablespoon Chinese light/thin regular soy sauce
- 1 tablespoon soy sauce wheat-free replacements, such as Dr. Bronner's or Braggs Liquid Aminos; or wheat- and soy-free replacement, such as Coconut Secret Coconut Aminos
- 2 teaspoon teriyaki sauce and 1 teaspoon water
- 1 teaspoon Maggi Seasoning

SOY SAUCE, KOREAN/GANJANG/KANJANG (medium-bodied) – 1 tablespoon
- 1 tablespoon Japanese-style all-purpose dark soy sauce (saltier)
- 1 tablespoon Chinese light/thin regular soy sauce (saltier and less sweet)

SOY SAUCE, MALAYSIAN/KICAP CAIR (light soy sauce) – 1 tablespoon
- 1 tablespoon Chinese or Japanese all-purpose regular soy sauce

SOY SAUCE, MALAYSIAN/KICAP HITAM (dark sweet soy sauce) – 1 tablespoon
- 1 tablespoon Indonesian thick sweet soy sauce/*kecap manis*

SOY SAUCE, MALAYSIAN/KICAP PEKAT (dark soy sauce) – 1 tablespoon
- 1 tablespoon Indonesian all-purpose soy sauce/*kecap asin*
- 1 tablespoon Chinese dark/black soy sauce (thinner and less salty)

SOY SAUCE, MUSHROOM (dark soy sauce infused with nameko or shiitake mushrooms) – 1 tablespoon
- 1 tablespoon dark soy sauce plus a pinch of sugar or drop of honey

SOY SAUCE, SWEET See KECAP MANIS

SOY SAUCE, THAI SWEET BLACK/NAM PLA SIIW/SIEW DAM – 1 tablespoon
- 1 tablespoon Indonesian thick sweet soy sauce/*kecap manis* (thicker)
- 1 tablespoon Chinese thick soy sauce/*jee yow* plus a little unsulphured molasses as a sweetener

SOY SAUCE, THAI THIN/SEE EIW/SI-EW – 1 tablespoon
- 1 tablespoon all-purpose Chinese light soy sauce

SOY SAUCE, VIETNAMESE/XI DAU
- 1 tablespoon all-purpose Chinese or Japanese light soy sauce

SOY SAUCE, WHITE/YIN BAI JIANG/SHIROJOYU – 1 tablespoon
- 2 teaspoons all-purpose soy sauce plus 1 teaspoon water

SPROUTS See SHOOTS AND SPROUTS

SQUASH, ASIAN (bitter melon, bottle gourd, angled loofah/Chinese okra, fuzzy melon/hairy melon, winter melon/wax gourd) – 1 pound
- 1 pound chayote/mirliton, marrow, large deseeded zucchini, or other summer squash (adjust the cooking time accordingly)

SQUID, FRESH RAW – 1 pound
- 1 pound cuttlefish (more tender)
- 1 pound baby octopus (less tender)

SQUID INK, CANNED OR FRESH – 1 tablespoon
- 1 tablespoon fresh cuttlefish ink

SRIRACHA See THAI HOT CHILI SAUCE

SRIRACHA SALT – 1 cup
Make Your Own Mix 1 cup kosher salt with 1/4 cup Sriracha sauce and spread in a thin layer on a parchment- or foil-lined baking sheet. Bake in a preheated 200°F oven until dry, 2 to 3 hours, then cool and pulse in a food processor until finely ground. Store in a tightly sealed container in a cool, dry place; it will keep for several weeks.

STAR ANISE (Chinese seasoning) – 1 whole star (8 points)
- 3/4 teaspoon crushed or broken star anise pieces
- 1/2 teaspoon ground star anise
- 3/4 teaspoon anise seeds (crushed with the side of a knife)
- 1/2 teaspoon ground anise or fennel
- 1/2 teaspoon Chinese five-spice powder (for savory dishes)

STAR ANISE, GROUND – 1 teaspoon
- 2 whole star anise, crushed; or 1 1/2 teaspoons broken pieces

- ⮞ 1 1/2 teaspoons anise or fennel seeds, ground in a pepper mill or spice/coffee grinder
- ⮞ 1 teaspoon ground anise
- ⮞ 1 teaspoon Chinese five-spice powder (for savory dishes)

STICKY RICE *See RICE, CHINESE BLACK, STICKY/FORBIDDEN; RICE, STICKY/SWEET/GLUTINOUS; RICE, THAI STICKY BLACK; RICE, THAI STICKY WHITE*

STOCK, CHICKEN OR MEAT (flavorful cooking liquid) – 1 cup

- ⮞ 1 cup liquid or broth saved from poaching or cooking chicken or meat (save and freeze the liquid until there is sufficient amount)
- ⮞ 2/3 cup canned reduced-sodium chicken or beef broth (or boxed no-salt chicken or beef stock) diluted with 1/3 cup water
- ⮞ 1/2 teaspoon chicken or beef instant stock/bouillon granules dissolved in 1 cup hot water
- ⮞ 1/2 teaspoon vegetarian chicken or beef broth/stock powder dissolved in 1 cup hot water
- ⮞ 1/2 cube reduced-sodium chicken or beef bouillon dissolved in 1 cup hot water
- ⮞ 1/2 teaspoon concentrated stock base paste, such as Bovril or Better than Bouillon, dissolved in 1 cup hot water
- ⮞ 1/2 teaspoon yeast extract, such as Marmite or Vegemite, dissolved in 1 cup hot water
- ⮞ Seasoning packet from a 3-ounce beef-flavored instant ramen noodle package dissolved in 1 cup hot water
- ⮞ 1 cup mushroom stock made from porcini mushroom–flavored bouillon granules or wild mushroom bouillon granules
- ⮞ 1 cup plain salted water

STOCK, FISH – 1 cup

- ⮞ 1 cup hot water plus 1/2 teaspoon instant fish bouillon granules, or 1/2 cube fish or shrimp-flavored bouillon, or 1/2 to 3/4 teaspoon seafood base or fish glaze, or 1/3 (1 1/2-ounce) package concentrated seafood stock

- 1 scant teaspoon dried bonito flakes simmered in 1 cup water a few minutes, then strained
- 1/2- to 1-inch square kombu/kelp added to 1 cup hot water and gently heated until the water is flavorful, 3 or 4 minutes; remove from heat and remove kombu (do not let boil)
- 1/3 cup bottled clam juice diluted with 2/3 cup water, vegetable broth, or dry white wine
- 1 cup boxed seafood cooking stock (diluted with water, if desired)
- Liquid from water-packed canned fish plus water to make 1 cup

Make Your Own Wash shrimp shells and heads, lobster shells, or fish heads and bones (gills removed) under cold running water, then place in a saucepan, and barely cover with water. Bring to a gentle boil and simmer, covered, for 20 to 30 minutes. Cool, strain, then measure 1 cup.

STRAW MUSHROOMS, FRESH – 8 ounces
- 1 (4-ounce) can straw mushrooms, drained and rinsed
- 8 ounces fresh enoki, oyster, or white button mushrooms

SUDACHI (Japanese lime-like citrus) – 1
- 1 kabosu or yuzu (larger; for juice and zest)
- 1 Key lime or small lemon (for juice and zest)
- Fresh or bottled yuzu juice (for juice)

SUGAR, BLACK See JAPANESE BLACK SUGAR

SUGAR, BROWN ROCK/SLAB/PIAN TANG/PEEN TONG (Chinese large-crystal sugar) – 1 (5 x 1-inch slab) (3 1/4 ounces coarsely grated or finely chopped)
- 1/2 cup firmly packed dark brown sugar plus 1 teaspoon unsulphured molasses

SUGAR, COCONUT PALM See JAGGERY

SUGAR, PALM See JAGGERY

SUGAR, ROCK See SUGAR, BROWN ROCK; SUGAR, YELLOW/CLEAR ROCK

SUGAR, SANDING/PEARL (extra-large-crystal cane or beet sugar) – 1 ounce
- 1 ounce Asian rock sugar, coarsely grated or finely chopped
- 1 ounce sugar pearls or sugar cubes, coarsely crushed
- 1 tablespoon Turbinado/semi-refined sugar

SUGAR, YELLOW/CLEAR ROCK/BING TANG/DUONG PHEN (large-crystal Asian sugar) – 1-inch crystal piece (scant 1/2-ounce) coarsely grated or finely chopped See also SUGAR, BROWN ROCK
- 1 tablespoon granulated or turbinado sugar

SUMO/DEKOPON (Japanese sweet hybrid orange) – 1
- 1 sweet satsuma orange

SUSHI DIPPING SAUCE (Japanese) – 1/4 cup
Make Your Own Combine 3 tablespoons water, 3 tablespoons Japanese soy sauce/*shoyu*, and 1 tablespoon mirin in a small saucepan. Simmer for 1 minute, then cool to room temperature.

SUSHI MESHI DRESSING (Japanese sushi rice seasoning) – 1/2 cup
- 1/2 cup Japanese seasoned rice vinegar (for sprinkling on hot rice)
- 1/2 cup instant powdered sushi vinegar (for sprinkling on hot rice)

SWEET-AND-SOUR SAUCE See CHINESE SWEET-AND-SOUR SAUCE

T

TAEYANGCHO RED PEPPER PASTE See KOREAN CHILI BEAN PASTE

TAIWANESE LETTUCE/CELTUCE/STEM LETTUCE/WO SUN/A-CHOY – 8 ounces
- 8 ounces celery or thin peeled broccoli stems (for stems)
- 8 ounces Romaine lettuce (for tops)

TAKNOTSUME (Japanese red Hawk Claw chili) – 1
- 1 cayenne or Tabasco chili

TAMARI (Japanese naturally fermented/traditionally brewed dense soy sauce) – 1 tablespoon *See also SOY SAUCE*
- 1 tablespoon tamari soy sauce (contains wheat but naturally brewed and without additives)
- 1 tablespoon wheat-free tamari, such as Crystal, Eden, San-J, or Westbrae tamari
- 1 tablespoon Japanese premium whole-bean organic soy sauce/ *marudaizu,* or *marudaizu*-grade soy sauce
- 1 tablespoon gluten-free soy sauce, such as LaChoy or San-J gluten-free
- 1 tablespoon reduced-sodium/lower-sodium tamari or soy sauce
- 1 tablespoon Bragg Liquid Aminos or Raw Coconut Aminos
- 1 1/2 teaspoons Maggi Seasoning
- Small pinch ground dulse seaweed

TAMARIND CONCENTRATE/EXTRACT/PASTE/PULP/IMLI (souring agent) – 1 tablespoon
- 1 dried tamarind slice (for curries, soups, and stews; discard before serving)
- 1 tablespoon pomegranate molasses

- ☞ 1 teaspoon molasses or brown sugar dissolved in 1 1/2 tablespoons lemon or lime juice (or 1 1/2 teaspoons lime juice plus 1/2 teaspoon Worcestershire sauce)
- ☞ 2 or 3 chopped pitted prunes, dried apricots, or Medjool dates, pureed with 1 tablespoon lemon juice until smooth, then measured

TAMARIND LEAVES (Asian souring agent) – 1 ounce fresh or frozen
- ☞ 1 ounce chopped fresh sorrel

TAMARIND PASTE (souring agent) – 1 tablespoon
- ☞ 1 to 2 tablespoons rice wine vinegar, or lime juice plus a pinch of brown sugar

TAMARIND PUREE (souring agent) – 1 cup
- ☞ 8 ounces (8 to 10) peeled tamarind pods, soaked in boiling water until softened, 1 to 2 hours; strain the pulp and discard the solids
- ☞ 1/2 cup (3 1/2 ounces) thawed frozen tamarind pulp, blended with 1/2 cup water; strain and discard the solids
- ☞ 1/4 cup (1 3/4 ounces) tamarind paste/concentrate, blended with 1 cup boiling water until smooth; strain and discard the solids

TAMARIND SAUCE (souring agent) – 1/2 cup
- ☞ 1 tablespoon tamarind concentrate added to 1/2 cup just-boiled water

TAMARIND WATER (souring agent) – 1 cup medium-strength
- ☞ 1 1/2 tablespoons tamarind paste, dissolved in 1 cup hot water

Make Your Own Soak 1 ounce (1 by 1 1/2-inch piece) compressed tamarind (or 6 cracked and peeled tamarind pods) in 1 1/2 cups boiling water until softened, 15 minutes or more. Strain and discard the solids. (For thick tamarind water, simmer the tamarind in the water until reduced by half and then strain.)

TANDOORI COLORING/TANDOORI RANG (Indian seasoning and coloring agent) – 1 teaspoon
- ☞ 1 tablespoon mild/sweet Hungarian or Spanish paprika (for coloring only)

☞ 1 tablespoon ground Madras turmeric, toasted in a dry skillet until fragrant (for coloring only)

☞ 1 drop red food coloring (for coloring only)

TANDOORI SEASONING (Indian spice blend) – 1 tablespoon

☞ 1/4 teaspoon each ground cumin (preferably roasted), ground coriander (preferably roasted), ground ginger (preferably roasted), mild paprika, turmeric, and ground cayenne pepper, plus salt to taste (optional)

☞ 1 tablespoon mild curry powder

TANGERINE/MANDARIN PEEL, DRIED/GOM PEI/TSEN PEI/CHEN PI/ GAW PAE (Chinese and Vietnamese seasoning)

☞ 1 (2-inch-long) strip orange zest, removed with a vegetable peeler, or 1/4 teaspoon grated fresh orange zest will substitute for 1 (1-inch-wide) piece dried tangerine peel

Make Your Own Arrange tangerine peels (preferably organic) on a rack and set in the sun, covered by a food umbrella or tented cheesecloth, until hard and dry. Alternatively, microwave on High for about 2 minutes, sandwiched between paper towels, or dry on a baking sheet in a preheated 200°F oven for about 1 hour. (If the oven has a top heating unit, place a large baking sheet as close to the heating unit as possible to deflect the heat, then place the baking sheet with the peels on a lower rack.) Store the peels in a small container and grind just before using.

TAPIOCA PEARLS – 1 tablespoon for cooking

☞ 1 tablespoon sago pearls

☞ 1 1/2 teaspoons quick-cooking tapioca (omit soaking and reduce cooking time)

TAPIOCA STARCH/FLOUR – 1 tablespoon for thickening

☞ 2 1/2 teaspoons quick-cooking tapioca ground in a spice/coffee grinder until powdery

☞ 1 1/2 teaspoons cornstarch or sweet/glutinous rice flour

- 1 1/4 teaspoons potato starch
- 2 teaspoons arrowroot powder
- 1 tablespoon all-purpose flour (cook for at least 3 minutes after thickening)

TAPIOCA, GRANULAR/QUICK-COOKING – 1 tablespoon for thickening

- 2 tablespoons small pearl tapioca, soaked in 1/4 cup milk or water until the liquid is completely absorbed, about 12 hours
- 1 1/2 tablespoons tapioca starch
- 1 1/2 tablespoons sago starch
- 1 1/2 teaspoons sweet/glutinous rice flour
- 2 teaspoon arrowroot powder (separates when frozen)

TARE (Japanese marinade and glaze) See TERIYAKI SAUCE

TARO CHIPS – 8 ounces

Make Your Own Slice the peeled taro root into paper-thin slices and toss with olive oil (plus salt and seasoning, if desired). Spread in a single layer on parchment-lined baking sheets and bake in a preheated 350°F oven until crisp, 15 to 20 minutes, rotating the pans, and flipping the chips halfway through.

TARO LEAVES/DASHEEN LEAVES/LUAU LEAVES/DAHEEN (green vegetable) – 1 pound

- 1 pound Swiss chard, beet greens, or spinach (shorten the cooking time accordingly)

TARO ROOT/ARBI/COCOYAM/GABI/WOO TAU (starchy vegetable) – 1 pound

- 1 pound eddo/malanga (moister)
- 1 pound fresh or frozen yucca root/cassava pieces
- 1 pound Yukon Gold or Yellow Finn potatoes (for the 7- to 8-inch taro)
- 1 pound small waxy boiling potatoes, such as Red Bliss (for the 2- to 3-inch Japanese baby taro/gabi)

TARO STEM/BAC HA/ZUIKI (Vietnamese and Cambodian green crispy vegetable) – 1 cup peeled and sliced
- 1 cup shredded iceberg lettuce

TATSOI/SPOON MUSTARD/CHINESE FLAT CABBAGE/TAI GU CHOY – 1 pound
- 1 pound baby spinach, baby arugula, young mizuna, young horse-radish leaves, or tender young mustard greens torn into pieces (for salad)
- 1 pound curly spinach, green chard, mustard greens with center rib discarded, baby bok choy, or baby Shanghai bok choy (for cooking)

TEA, GREEN – 1 cup brewed
- 1 cup organic tulsi tea (caffeine-free; higher in antioxidants)
- I cup light-roast yaupon tea (less-bitter taste, less tannin, less caffeine)
- 1 cup dandelion tea (use dried leaves; caffeine-free)
- 1 cup New Jersey Tea/*Ceanothus americanus* (use fresh or dried leaves; resembles green tea in flavor; caffeine-free)

TEMPEH, FRESH OR FROZEN (fermented soybean) – 1 pound
- 2 (8-ounce) packages Organic Savory Baked Tofu/baked bean curd (spicy or smoked seasoned; softer texture)
- 1 pound firm tofu, weighted a few hours, then blotted dry and sliced crosswise (softer texture; less flavorful)
- 1 pound seitan (chewier)

TEMPURA BATTER/KOROMO (Japanese) – 1 cup
Make Your Own Gently stir together 1 cup tempura flour (or 1 cup rice or cake flour), preferably chilled; 1/2 teaspoon salt; and 1 cup ice-cold sparkling water (or club soda or light beer). (Don't overmix; use immediately.)

TEMPURA DIPPING SAUCE/TENTSUYU (Japanese) – 1/3 cup
- 1/4 cup dashi (or light vegetable or chicken broth) plus 1 tablespoon each mirin and Japanese soy sauce/*shoyu*, brought to a boil then cooled

- 1/4 cup Japanese soy sauce/*shoyu*, 2 tablespoons mild vinegar, 2 teaspoons sugar, and 1 or 2 teaspoons finely grated ginger, stirred until the sugar dissolves
- 1 1/2 tablespoons Memmi noodle soup base, such as Kikkoman, mixed with 1/4 cup water

TEMPURA FLOUR/TENPURA KO (Japanese) – 1 cup
- 3/4 cup plus 2 tablespoons cake flour and 2 tablespoons cornstarch or potato starch

TENTSUYU *See TEMPURA DIPPING SAUCE*

TERASI/TRASI (Indonesian and Malaysian seasoning) *See SHRIMP PASTE, FERMENTED*

TERIYAKI SAUCE/TERIYAKI SOSU/TARÉ (Japanese marinade and glaze) – 1/3 cup
Make Your Own Bring 2 tablespoons each Japanese dark soy sauce, mirin, and saké (or dry sherry) to a boil in the microwave, or in a small saucepan over medium heat, then cool. (For a sweeter sauce, add 1 teaspoon sugar; for a thicker sauce add 1 1/2 teaspoons sugar and simmer until syrupy.)
Or
Heat 1/4 cup soy sauce and 2 tablespoons sugar (or honey) in the microwave until the sugar dissolves, 10 to 20 seconds.

THAI BASIL *See BASIL, THAI*

THAI CHILI/LONG CHILI/PRIK CHI FAA, FRESH OR DRIED – 1
- 1 fresh or dried de árbol, japonés, small serrano, tien tsin, or cayenne chili
- 1/4 to 1/2 teaspoon Thai red pepper flakes or hot red pepper flakes
- 1/8 teaspoon each ground cayenne pepper and paprika

THAI CHILI PEPPER/PRIK KI NU *See BIRD'S EYE CHILI*

THAI CHILI FLAKES/POWDER – 1/2 cup

Make Your Own Toast 1 cup dried Thai chilis in a dry skillet over medium heat, stirring frequently, until slightly darker, 2 to 3 minutes (or in a preheated 350°F oven until puffed, about 5 minutes). Cool, remove the stems, then pulse in a food processor into coarse flakes or process to a powder. (For less heat remove the seeds and veins; wear plastic gloves and avoid inhaling the fumes.)

THAI CHILI VINEGAR/NAM SOM – (pad thai condiment) – 1/2 cup

- 1/2 cup rice vinegar, 2 to 3 tablespoons sugar, and a few thin slices of serrano chili

THAI CURRY POWDER/PONG GARI – 1 tablespoon

- 1 tablespoon mild Madras curry powder

THAI DIPPING SAUCE/NAM PRIK See NAM PRIK

THAI FISH SAUCE/NAM PLA (salty liquid seasoning) – 1 tablespoon

- 1 tablespoon Vietnamese fish sauce/*nuoc nam/nuoc mam* (less pungent), or Vietnamese premium sauce from the first extraction/*nuoc mam nhi* or *nuoc mam cot* (bolder flavor)
- 1 tablespoon Korean fish sauce/*saengseon*, Japanese fish sauce/*shottsuru*, or Filipino fish sauce/*patis*
- 1 tablespoon Vietnamese vegetarian fish sauce/*nuoc mam au chay*
- 1 tablespoon anchovy essence/syrup
- 2 teaspoons anchovy paste mixed with 1/2 teaspoon soy sauce or Maggi Seasoning
- 1 tablespoon oyster sauce
- 1 scant tablespoon light soy sauce plus a little salt

THAI FISH SAUCE WITH CHILIS/NAM PLA PRIK – 2/3 (scant) cup

Make Your Own Stir 1/4 cup minced fresh Thai chilis (including seeds) into 1/2 cup fish sauce/*nam pla*. Store, tightly covered, in the refrigerator for up to 3 months. (Wear plastic gloves when handling the chilis.)

THAI GINGER *See GALANGAL, GREATER*

THAI GINGER, WILD/GRACHAI/KRACHAI/LESSER GINGER – 1 ounce
 ⮡ 1 ounce regular ginger

THAI HOT CHILI SAUCE/SRIRACHA SAUCE/SOT SIRACHA/TUONG OT SRIRACHA – 1 teaspoon
 ⮡ 1/2 teaspoon each American-made Sriracha sauce/rooster sauce (thicker, stronger, less sweet) and Thai sweet chili sauce/*nam jim kai*
 ⮡ 1 teaspoon sambal oelek sweetened with a little sugar
 ⮡ 3/4 teaspoon ketchup plus 1/4 teaspoon Louisiana-style hot sauce, such as Tabasco or Crystal
 ⮡ 1/2 to 1 teaspoon Sriracha dry seasoning (for cooking)
 ⮡ 1/4 to 1/2 teaspoon ground cayenne pepper (for cooking; lacks flavor)

THAI NOODLES, CLEAR TRANSPARENT/WUN SEN *See NOODLES, CEL-LOPHANE*

THAI NOODLES, THIN, FLAT RICE/PAD THAI NOODLES, DRIED OR SEMI-DRIED/SEN LEK/BAH PHO/PHAT THAI – 1 pound *See also NOO-DLES, THIN, FLAT RICE*
 ⮡ 1 pound fresh or 12 ounces dried fettuccine, prepared according to the package directions
 ⮡ 8 to 12 ounces dried, or 1 pound fresh, Vietnamese *banh pho,* Chinese *sha ha fun* or *chow fun,* Filipino *pancit luglug,* or other flat 1/8-inch or 1/4-inch rice noodles
 ⮡ 1 pound fresh or 8 to 12 ounces dried thin, flat brown rice noodles, prepared according to the package directions

THAI NOODLES, THIN RICE, DRIED/KWAY TIO/SEN MEE/KANOM CHINE – 1 pound
 ⮡ 1 pound Thai rice sticks/*sen yai,* Chinese rice vermicelli/*mi fen/so fun;* Japanese *mai fun;* Vietnamese *bun and bahn hoi;* or Filipino *pancit bihon*

THAI NOODLES, WHEAT/BA MEE, FRESH OR FROZEN – 1 pound
⇨ 1 pound fresh or 12 ounces dried Chinese egg noodles, or Japanese yakisoba or fresh-frozen ramen noodles

THAI RICE See RICE, THAI BLACK STICKY; RICE, THAI JASMINE; RICE, THAI JASMINE RED/PURPLE; RICE, THAI WHITE STICKY

THAI RICE, GROUND ROASTED See RICE POWDER, ROASTED

THAI ROASTED RED CHILI PASTE/CHILI JAM/NAM PRIK PAO – 1 tablespoon
⇨ 1 tablespoon chili-garlic sauce
⇨ 2 teaspoons vegetable oil, 1 teaspoon granulated sugar, and 1 teaspoon chili powder

THAI SAUCE BASE – 1/4 cup
⇨ 3 tablespoons fish sauce/*nam pla*, 1 tablespoon lime juice, 1 tablespoon brown sugar, and 1/8 teaspoon crushed red pepper flakes, stirred until the sugar dissolves

THAI SEVEN-SPICE POWDER – 1 teaspoon
⇨ 1 teaspoon Chinese five-spice powder

THAI SHRIMP PASTE/KAPI See SHRIMP PASTE, FERMENTED

THAI SOY SAUCE See SOY SAUCE, THAI THIN

THAI SWEET BLACK SOY SAUCE See SOY SAUCE, THAI SWEET BLACK

THAI SWEET CHILI-GARLIC SAUCE/NAM JIM KRATIEM – 1/2 cup
Make Your Own Simmer 1 cup distilled white vinegar, 1/2 cup sugar, and 1 teaspoon salt until syrupy, 10 to 15 minutes. Remove from the heat and add 1 teaspoon minced fresh Thai chili and 1/2 teaspoon minced garlic. Cool and transfer to an airtight container. (The sauce will thicken further as it cools and will keep, refrigerated, for up to a few months.)

THAI YELLOW BEAN PASTE/DAU JIAO/TAO JIAW See *VIETNAMESE YELLOW BEAN SAUCE*

TIGER LILY BUDS See *LILY BUDS*

TIGER NUTS/CHUFA (small tubers) See *CHESTNUTS*

TINAPA (Filipino brined smoked fish) – 1/4 cup
- 1/4 cup dried shrimp or bonita flakes plus a dash of smoked paprika

TOFU/BEAN CURD, FRESH – 1 pound
- 1 pound tempeh (stronger flavor)
- 1 pound Indian paneer/panir or Latin American queso blanco/fresco (diced for adding to savory dishes)

TOFU, BROILED/YAKIDOFU – 1 pound
- 1 pound firm or extra-firm tofu, drained and grilled each side over high heat, preferably charcoal

TOFU, DEEP-FRIED/ABURAGÉ – 1 pound
- 1 pound sliced firm tofu, weighted, patted dry, then deep-fried until golden brown, 3 to 4 minutes (drain on paper towels and cool)
- 1 pound *atsu-agé* or *nama-agé* (thicker sheets)

TOFU, DRIED/FOO JOOK – 1 pound
- 1 pound firm or extra-firm tofu, baked at 375°F until dry, about 25 minutes (or wrapped in a non-terry cotton dishtowel or paper towels and microwaved on High in 30-second increments for about 2 minutes)

TOFU, FERMENTED/DOUFU RU/FUYU/SUFU – 1 pound
- 1 pound firm or extra-firm tofu, sliced or cubed, then marinated for 1 to 2 days in miso or soy sauce
- 1 pound mild French or Greek feta cheese, crumbled

TOFU, FREEZE-DRIED/KOYADOFU – 1 pound
- ☞ 1 pound firm or extra-firm tofu, rinsed, weighted for 1 to 2 hours, then frozen in plastic wrap for 8 to 12 hours (rinse in water after thawing)

TOFU, PRESSED/DOUFU-KAN/TAU JUA/TAU KWA – 1 pound
- ☞ 1 pound extra-firm tofu, placed between 2 folded dishtowels and weighted until dry, 2 to 3 hours (use a heavy skillet or cutting board and canned goods for weights)
- ☞ 1 pound extra-firm tofu, cut into thin slices, placed on a paper-lined plate, and microwaved on Medium until dry, 4 to 6 minutes

TOFU, SILKEN/KINUGOSHI/SUI –DOUFU – 1 pound
- ☞ 1 pound soy yogurt

TOGARASHI See JAPANESE HOT RED CHILI

TONKATSU SAUCE (thick sauce for tonkatsu) – 1/3 cup
Make Your Own Stir 1 tablespoon Worcestershire sauce and 1 teaspoon dark soy sauce into 1/4 cup ketchup until thoroughly combined. (For a more pungent sauce, use 3 tablespoons Worcestershire sauce, 2 tablespoons ketchup, and 1 teaspoon soy sauce.)

TORIGARA BASE (Japanese chicken stock base) – 1 teaspoon
- ☞ 1 teaspoon reduced-sodium chicken bouillon cube, 1 envelope instant chicken broth or granules, 1/2 to 3/4 teaspoon chicken extract or soup base, or 2 teaspoons vegetarian-based chicken broth powder (all substitutions will be saltier)

TOYOMANSI See SOY SAUCE, FILIPINO CITRUS

TREE EAR See CLOUD EAR/BLACK TREE FUNGUS

TSAMPA (Tibetan roasted barley flour) – 1 cup
- ☞ 2/3 cup whole hulled/pot barley, whole hull-less barley, or pearl barley toasted in a dry skillet until golden, about 4 minutes. Cool, then grind in batches in a spice/coffee grinder until powdery.

**TURMERIC ROOT, FRESH OR FROZEN (Southeast Asian seasoning) –
1-inch piece or 1 tablespoon peeled and finely chopped or grated**
- 2 teaspoons grated dried turmeric rhizome (wear plastic gloves and be careful; turmeric stains are hard to remove)
- 1 teaspoon ground dried turmeric
- 1 tablespoon grated carrot plus 1/2 teaspoon each powdered turmeric and grated fresh ginger
- 2 teaspoons finely chopped fresh ginger
- 1 teaspoon powdered Alleppey turmeric (orange-yellow color; for flavor) or powdered Madras turmeric (bright yellow; for color)
- 1 1/2 teaspoons turmeric powder (for color)
- 1/4 teaspoon finely ground annatto seeds, achiote/Bijoi powder, or mild yellow curry powder (for color only)

TURMERIC ROOT POWDER/GROUND TURMERIC/HALDI (Indian coloring and flavoring spice) – 1 teaspoon
- 1 tablespoon packed fresh grated turmeric
- Small pinch of saffron, crushed dried safflower florets, or safflower stigmas/Mexican saffron/*azafrán* (for color)
- 1 teaspoon ground annatto seeds or achiote/Bijoi powder (for color)
- 2 teaspoons ground dried marigold petals, or whole dried marigold petals steeped in a little warm water 5 minutes (use the liquid for color and discard the petals)

TURMERIC, WHITE *See ZEDOARY*

TURNIPS *See JAPANESE TURNIPS*

U

UDO (Japanese white stalk vegetable) – 1 pound
- 1 pound fennel (bulb and thick green stalks)
- 1 pound white asparagus or celery plus a pinch of crushed fennel seeds

UDON See JAPANESE NOODLES, THICK WHEAT

UMAMI DUST (Japanese flavor-enhancing seasoning) – 1 ounce
- 1/2 ounce crumbled dried kombu/kelp (1/2 sheet), 1/2 ounce dried shiitake caps (about 5 large), and 3 tablespoons dried bonito flakes, ground until fine

UMEBOSHI (Japanese salt-pickled dried plum) – 1 large (1 tablespoon pitted and mashed)
- 1 quickly pickled salted plum/*shio-hikaeme umeboshi* (juicier, with less salt)
- 1 Chinese pickled plum/*suan mei* or salted dried plum/*li hing mui/ hua mei*
- 2 teaspoons jarred umeboshi puree/paste/*bainiku/neri-ume*
- 1 1/2 teaspoons umeboshi plum vinegar/*ume su* (much saltier)
- 2 or 3 tiny plum paste balls/*umeboshi-san*

UMEBOSHI PASTE/BAINIKU – 1 ounce
- 1 ounce Japanese dried, salt-pickled plum/*umeboshi* or Chinese pickled plum/*suanmel*, ground with a mortar and pestle until smooth

UMEBOSHI VINEGAR/UME SU – 1 tablespoon
- 1 1/2 teaspoons lemon juice and 1 1/2 teaspoons Japanese soy sauce or tamari

- ☞ 1 (scant) tablespoon red rice vinegar or red wine vinegar plus a few drops of soy sauce
- ☞ 1 tablespoon cider vinegar plus a pinch of table salt
- ☞ 1 tablespoon sherry vinegar

URAD DAL FLOUR (Indian) – 1 cup

- ☞ 1 1/4 cups split and husked black lentils, roasted in a dry skillet until slightly aromatic, 5 to 10 minutes, then finely ground in a food mill, or in batches in a coffee/spice grinder

V

VIETNAMESE BASIL/RAU HUYNG See BASIL, THAI

VIETNAMESE CARAMEL SAUCE/NUOC MAU – 1 tablespoon
- 1 tablespoon molasses

VIETNAMESE CHILI SALT/MUOI TIEU – 1/4 cup
- 3 to 4 red Thai bird chilies and 2 to 3 tablespoons Kosher salt pulverized in a coffee/spice grinder until reduced to a powder

VIETNAMESE CHILI SAUCE/TUONG OT TOI – 1 tablespoon
- 1 tablespoon sambal oelek, harissa, Sriracha, Sichuan chili sauce, or hot pepper sauce, such as Tabasco or Crystal

VIETNAMESE CORIANDER See VIETNAMESE MINT

VIETNAMESE DIPPING SAUCE/TUONG GUNG – 1/2 cup
- 1/4 cup each Vietnamese fish sauce/*nuoc nam*, fresh lime juice, and superfine sugar stirred together until the sugar dissolves
- 2 tablespoons each unseasoned rice vinegar, water, and fresh lime juice; plus 1 teaspoon each chili-garlic paste (or Chinese chili-garlic sauce), sugar, and soy sauce stirred together until the sugar dissolves

VIETNAMESE FISH SAUCE/NUOC NAM/NUOC MAM – 1 tablespoon
- 1 tablespoon premium (gluten-free) *nuoc nam* made with the first pressing (*cot, nhi, thuong hang, phu quoc*)
- 1 tablespoon Thai fish sauce/*nam pla*, Korean fish sauce/*saengseon*, Japanese fish sauce/*shottsuru*, or Filipino fish sauce/*patis*
- 1 tablespoon vegetarian fish sauce/*nuoc nam chay*
- 2 teaspoons anchovy essence/syrup mixed with a few drops light soy sauce

☞ 1/2 teaspoon Worcestershire sauce

VIETNAMESE MINT/LAKSA LEAF/RAU RAM/PHAK PHAI/DAUN KES-OM/DAUN LAKSA, FRESH – 1 tablespoon chopped
☞ 1 1/2 teaspoons each chopped fresh cilantro and spearmint (or peppermint)
☞ 1 1/2 teaspoons each chopped fresh cilantro and lemon balm leaves (or lemon basil)
☞ 1 tablespoon chopped domestic garden cilantro going to seed (starting to flower)

VIETNAMESE NOODLES, CELLOPHANE/MUNG BEAN/BEAN THREADS/ BUN TAU See NOODLES, CELLOPHANE

VIETNAMESE NOODLES, MEDIUM WHITE RICE/BÁNH PHO/NU TIEU – 1 pound
☞ 1 pound fresh or 8 to 12 ounces dried Chinese, Thai, or other 1/4-inch linguine-type rice noodles

VIETNAMESE PICKLED LEEKS/CU KIEU – 1 cup
☞ Cornichons or other mild cucumber pickles

VIETNAMESE SHRIMP PASTE/MAM TOM See SHRIMP PASTE, FERMENTED

VIETNAMESE SOY SAUCE See SOY SAUCE, VIETNAMESE

VIETNAMESE SWEET-AND-SOUR DIPPING SAUCE/NUOC CHAM – scant 1/2 cup
Make Your Own 1/4 cup each sugar, Vietnamese fish sauce/*nuoc nam*, and lime juice, plus 1 small minced garlic clove, and 1 minced fresh Thai or cayenne chili stirred until the sugar dissolves
Or
1/3 cup chili-garlic sauce, 1 tablespoon Vietnamese fish sauce/*nuoc nam*, and 1 tablespoon lime juice stirred until combined (for *nuoc nam gung*, add finely chopped fresh ginger)

VIETNAMESE SWEET CHILI SAUCE/TUONG OT NGOT – scant 2/3 cup

- ⇨ 2/3 cup Thai sweet chili sauce/dipping sauce for chicken/*nam jim kai*
- ⇨ 3 tablespoons sambal oelek and 2 tablespoons unseasoned rice vinegar stirred into 1/3 cup mild honey

VIETNAMESE YELLOW BEAN SAUCE/TUONG OT/TUONG CU DA – 1 tablespoon

- ⇨ 1 tablespoon *awase* miso (a mixture of white and red miso)
- ⇨ 1 scant tablespoon Chinese yellow/brown soybean paste/*hugan jiang* or Thai yellow bean paste/*tao jiaw* thinned with a few drops of water
- ⇨ 1 1/2 teaspoons each Japanese light and dark miso

VIETNAMESE YOGURT/SUA CHUA/DA UA – 1 cup

- ⇨ 1 (3.5-ounce) can sweetened condensed milk stirred into 3/4 cup plain Greek-style yogurt until thoroughly incorporated (store, tightly covered, in the refrigerator; it will last for up to 2 weeks)

W

WAKAME/HOSHI WAKAME/MIYUK, DRIED *(Japanese dark green sea vegetable) – 1 ounce*
- 1 ounce freeze-dried, salt-covered wakame/*yutōshi shiozo wakame* (soak in cool water for 10 minutes, then rinse thoroughly to remove excess salt)
- 1 ounce refrigerated finely shredded wakame/*mozuku wakame* (soak in cool water for 10 to 15 minutes, or add directly to soups)
- 1/2 ounce shredded or flaked instant wakame/*katto wakame* (soak in cool water for 1 to 3 minutes, or add directly to soup; it swells to several times its original volume: 1 tablespoon makes 1/2 cup/1 1/2 ounces)
- 1 ounce bite-size wakame/*fueru wakame* (soak in cool water for 5 minutes)
- 1 ounce lighter-colored more delicate wakame/*ito wakame* (soak in cool water for 15 minutes)
- 2/3 ounce dried alaria/winged kelp (saltier and chewier, soak in cool water for 20 to 60 minutes)
- 1 ounce dried arame (long, black delicate strands; milder flavor; rinse, then soak in cool water for 5 to 10 minutes)
- 1 ounce dulse sheets or flakes (saltier; no soaking required)
- 1 ounce dried *nikombu* (kombu for eating; not dashi kombu; stronger flavor; soak in cool water for 5 to 10 minutes)
- 2 cups lightly packed fresh or frozen chopped chard or kale (cook until tender)
- 4 to 5 cups coarsely chopped fresh young spinach leaves (blanch for 1 minute, refresh in ice water, then squeeze out excess water)

WAKAME POWDER *(Japanese condiment)*
Make Your Own Cut dried wakame into small pieces and toast in a dry skillet, stirring constantly, until very crisp, about 5 minutes. Crumble

or grind into a powder (use a mortar and pestle or a rolling pin sleeved in plastic). Store in an airtight container in a cool, dark cupboard; it will last for up to 1 year.

WASABI/HON WASABI (Japanese horseradish) – 2-ounce root (1 tablespoon freshly grated)
- ☞ 1 or more tablespoons wasabi paste/*neriwasabi*
- ☞ 1 tablespoon wasabi powder/*konawasabi* stirred into 2 teaspoons cold water and left covered for 5 to 10 minutes to develop the flavor

WASABI, POWDERED – 1 teaspoon
- ☞ 1 teaspoon horseradish or mustard powder

WASABI, PREPARED – 1 teaspoon
- ☞ 1 teaspoon wasabi powder mixed with 1 scant teaspoon cold water, then left, covered, 10 to 15 minutes to develop the flavor
- ☞ 1 teaspoon fresh horseradish (or strained bottled horseradish) plus a touch of green food coloring
- ☞ 1 teaspoon mustard powder, 1/2 teaspoon vinegar, 1/4 teaspoon oil, and 1/8 teaspoon salt mixed together until smooth, then left, covered, for 10 to 15 minutes to develop the flavor

WATER CHESTNUT STARCH/POWDER/MA TIE FUN (Asian thickening agent) – 1 tablespoon
- ☞ 1 tablespoon lotus root starch or cornstarch

WATER CHESTNUTS/MAH TAI/HAEW/SHINGHDA, FRESH (Asian tuber vegetable) – 1 cup
- ☞ 1 cup canned water chestnuts, drained and rinsed (or briefly blanched in boiling water)
- ☞ 1 cup chopped fresh jícama
- ☞ 1 cup chopped cooked (or canned) lotus root
- ☞ 1 cup chopped cooked burdock root
- ☞ 1 cup small cooked sunchokes or large ones sliced or cubed (add at the end of cooking)

WATER SPINACH/KANGKONG/PAK BOONG/ONG CHOY/RAU MU-ONG/VLITA (Southeast Asian vegetable) – 1 bunch (about 2 pounds)
- 1 bunch sweet potato leaves, including stems (Only sweet potato leaves are edible; regular potato leaves are poisonous.)
- 1 1/2 bunches (about 1 1/2 pounds) regular mature spinach or Taiwan spinach, including stems

WHEAT STARCH/TANG FLOUR/TANG MIEN FUN/CHENG MIAN FEN (Chinese gluten-free flour and thickener) – 1/4 cup
- 1/4 cup cornstarch; potato starch, or tapioca starch

WHEAT STARCH SYRUP (Japanese natural sweetener) See MIZUAME

WILD LIME LEAF See KAFFIR LIME LEAF

WILD PEPPER LEAVES/WILD BETAL LEAVES/BAI CHAMPLUU/BO LA LOT/DAUN KADOK (Indian and Southeast Asian seasoning and food wrapper)
- Chinese broccoli leaves (for seasoning)
- Grape leaves, choy sum, young spinach leaves, butter lettuce leaves, or deveined collard greens cut into 3-inch squares (for wrapping) See also WRAPPERS FOR FOOD, VEGETABLE-BASED

WINE, YELLOW RICE See SHAOXING

WONTON CRISPS
Make Your Own Cut wonton wrappers in half diagonally, coat with cooking spray, and spread in a single layer on a baking sheet. Bake at 375°F oven until golden, 6 to 8 minutes, turning halfway through. Alternatively, fry the cut wrappers in 350°F oil until golden, about 30 seconds, then drain on paper towels. For sweet chips, sprinkle them with cinnamon sugar or plain sugar while still hot.

WONTON WRAPPERS – 1 pound
- 1 pound *siu mai* wrappers (round)

- 1 pound egg roll wrappers, cut into quarters (thicker)
- 1 pound rice paper or spring roll wrappers, cut to size (thinner)
- 1 pound fresh pasta, rolled thin and cut to size
- 1 pound fresh or thawed frozen bean curd skins/*yuba/wu pei/dou fu bao*, cut to size
- 8 to 12 ounces dried bean curd skins/tofu bamboo/tofu leather/ *doufu zhu*, soaked in hot water for 1 hour, then cut to size

Make Your Own Combine 2 cups all-purpose flour, 1/2 teaspoon salt, 1 large egg and 1/2 cup water. Knead the dough for at least 5 minutes until smooth, then let it rest for 30 minutes covered with a damp cloth. Roll the dough out very thinly, then cut it into 3-inch squares.

WOOD EAR FUNGUS See CLOUD EAR/BLACK TREE FUNGUS

WRAPPERS FOR FOOD, NON-EDIBLE (soak dried leaves in hot water until softened and pliable, 10 to 60 minutes, then drain and pat dry)
- Agave leaves
- Avocado leaves
- Bamboo leaves, fresh or dried (cut out the dried stem after softening)
- Banana leaves, fresh or thawed frozen, cut into pieces
- Breadfruit leaves
- Corn husks, fresh or dried (use several layers if necessary)
- Lotus leaves
- Maguey leaves
- Plantain leaves, cut into pieces
- Ti leaves, fresh
- Yuka leaves

WRAPPERS FOR FOOD, VEGETABLE-BASED (For thin leaves blanch in boiling water 10 seconds; for thick leaves, 1 to 5 minutes until softened; or microwave, covered, 2 to 3 minutes on High. If necessary, flatten the central rib or shave it to make it the same thickness as the rest of the leaf, or cut it out entirely)
- Large burdock leaves

- Cabbage leaves: green, napa, or Savoy
- Daikon or butternut squash slices (peeled, trimmed to create flat edges, then shaved into paper-thin strips)
- Young chaya leaves
- Fava leaves, preferably mature
- Fig leaves, usually Black Mission
- Grape leaves
- Greens: beet, choy sum, collard, kale, kohlrabi, young mallow, mustard, parsnip, Swiss chard, mature spinach, or turnip
- *Hoja santa* leaves
- *La-lot* leaves
- Lettuce leaves (large outer leaves): butterhead, crisphead, iceburg, looseleaf, or romaine (If necessary, soften briefly in the microwave or dip into boiling water.)
- Papaya leaves
- Perilla or shiso leaves
- Radicchio leaves
- Turmeric leaves
- Wild pepper leaves/*la-lot* leaves
- Zucchini slices (Trim large zucchini, cut into paper-thin lengthwise strips, sprinkle with salt, and let soften about 20 minutes. Rinse and pat dry. Alternatively, bake raw slices at 350°F until barely softened.)

X

XO SAUCE, VEGAN (Chinese spicy, seafood-based condiment) – 1 tablespoon
- 1 tablespoon vegetarian oyster sauce plus a few drops of chili oil (lacks seafood and mushroom taste)

Y

YAKISOBA NOODLES, DRIED – 3-ounce packet
☞ 1 (3-ounce) packet instant ramen noodles (thinner)

YAKISOBA SAUCE (Japanese stir-fry flavoring sauce) – 1 tablespoon
☞ 1 tablespoon Japanese brown sauce or tonkatsu sauce

YAKITORI SAUCE (Japanese grilling sauce and glaze) – 1 cup
☞ 1 cup heavy teriyaki sauce (or 1 1/2 cups thin teriyaki sauce, boiled until reduced to 1 cup)

YAM BEAN (tuberous vegetable) – 1 pound
☞ 1 pound jícama or Asian hard pears (for cooking, salads or pickling)
☞ 1 pound water chestnuts, fresh or canned (for cooking or salads; rinse or blanch the canned type)

YELLOW BEAN SAUCE See CHINESE YELLOW BEAN SAUCE; VIETNAMESE YELLOW BEAN SAUCE

YELLOW SOY BEANS, SALTED FERMENTED (Chinese cooking condiment) – 1 tablespoon
☞ 1 1/2 tablespoons Chinese yellow/brown bean sauce/*hugan jiang*, Thai yellow bean sauce/*tao jiew*, or Vietnamese yellow bean sauce/*tuong ot*
☞ 1 or 2 tablespoons Japanese all-purpose light miso (such as *genmai* or *shinshu*)

YOMOGI (Japanese green vegetable and seasoning for soba noodles)
☞ Fresh or dried mugwort/*ssuk*
☞ Tender wild mugwort/*Artemisia vulgaris*
☞ Arugula or watercress leaves (different flavor)

YUZU/MISHO YUZU (Japanese small tart citrus fruit) – 1
- ⮞ 1 or 2 *sudachi*
- ⮞ One-half Meyer lemon (less bitter)

YUZU JUICE – 1 tablespoon fresh, frozen, or bottled
- ⮞ 1 tablespoon *sudachi* juice (slightly more acidic)
- ⮞ erellee1 teaspoon each grapefruit, lemon, and lime juice
- ⮞ 2 1/2 teaspoons fresh lime juice plus 1/2 teaspoon fresh orange juice

YUZU ZEST – 1 teaspoon
- ⮞ 1/3 teaspoon dried yuzu peel, softened in 2 teaspoons warm water for 15 minutes, then finely chopped
- ⮞ 3/4 to 1 teaspoon yuzu powder
- ⮞ 1 to 2 teaspoons lemon zest or fully ripened Key lime zest

Z

ZEDOARY/WHITE TURMERIC/MANGO GINGER/AMBA HALDI (Indian and Southeast Asian seasoning) – 1 dried slice

- 1 slice dried galangal/*galanga* (add directly to a soup or stew without soaking)
- 1/4 to 1/2 teaspoon ground *zedoary* powder
- 1/8 to 1/4 teaspoon powdered *kencur*, Laos powder, or galangal paste
- Tiny pinch ground ginger
- 1 small piece fresh or thawed frozen galangal

Thank you for purchasing my book, dear reader.
I hope you will find it helpful.

Jean B. MacLeod

BIBLIOGRAPHY

Alford, Jeffrey, and Naomi Duguid. *Beyond the Great Wall: Recipes and Travels in the Other China*. New York: Artisan, 2008.

Aranas, Jennifer. *The Filipino-American Kitchen: Traditional Recipes, Contemporary Flavors*. North Clarendon, VT: Tuttle Publishing, 2006.

Belleme, Jan, and John Belleme. *Cooking with Japanese Foods*. Garden City Park, NY: Avery, 1993.

Bhattacharya, Rinku. *The Bengali Five Spice Chronicles: Exploring the Cuisine of Eastern India*. New York: Hippocrene Books, 2012.

Bhide, Monica. *Modern Spice: Inspired Indian Flavors for the Contemporary Kitchen*. New York: Simon & Schuster, 2009.

Bhumichitr, Vatcharin. *The Essential Thai Cookbook*. New York: Clarkson N. Potter, 1994.

Bladholm, Linda. *The Asian Grocery Store Demystified*. Los Angeles: Renaissance Books, 1999.

_____. *The Indian Grocery Store Demystified*. Los Angeles: Renaissance Books, 2000.

Brissenden, Rosemary. *Southeast Asian Food: Classic and Modern Dishes from Indonesia, Malaysia, Singapore, Thailand, Laos, Cambodia, and Vietnam*. 1st Periplus ed. Singapore: Periplus Editions. 2007.

Chun, Injoo, Jaewoon Lee, and Youngran Baek. *Authentic Recipes from Korea*. Singapore: Periplus, 2004.

Cost, Bruce. *Bruce Cost's Asian Ingredients: Buying and Cooking the Staple Foods of China, Japan and Southeast Asia*. New York: William Morrow, 1988.

Dahlen, Martha. *A Cook's Guide to Chinese Vegetables*. Hong Kong: Workman Press, 2000.

Danhi, Robert. *Southeast Asian Flavors: Adventures in Cooking the Foods of Thailand, Vietnam, Malaysia, & Singapore:* El Segundo: Mortar & Press, 2008.

Davidson, Alan. *The Oxford Companion to Food*. Oxford: Oxford University Press, 1999.

Fernandez, Rafi. *Indian, Chinese, Thai, and Asian: 1,000 Recipes*. London: Lorenz Books, 2009.

Grigson, Jane, and Charlotte Knox. *Exotic Fruits and Vegetables*. New York: Henry Holt, 1986.

Hachisu, Nancy Singleton. *Japanese Farm Food*. Kansas City, MO: Andrews McMeel Publishing, 2012.

Harlow, Jay. *Cuisines of Southeast Asia: Thai, Vietnamese, Indonesian, Burmese & More*. Santa Rosa, CA: Cole Group, 1987.

Hom, Ken. *Ken Hom's Chinese Kitchen: With a Consumer's Guide to Essential Ingredients*. New York: Hyperion, 1994.

Hosking, Richard. *A Dictionary of Japanese Food Ingredients & Culture*. Rutland, VT: Charles E. Tuttle, 1996.

Hoy, Sharon Wong. *Cuisine of China*. Hawthorne, CA: Benshaw Publications, 1982.

Hsiung, Deh-Ta. *The Chinese Kitchen*. 1st U.S. ed. New York: St. Martin's Press, 1999.

Hsiung, Deh-Ta, Becky Johnson, and Sallie Morris. *The Ultimate Thai and Asian Cookbook*. London: Lorenz Books, 2008.

Jaffrey, Madhur. *At Home with Madhur Jaffrey: Simple, Delectable Dishes from India, Pakistan, Bangladesh, and Sri Lanka*. New York: Alfred A. Knopf, 2010.

Kapoor, Sanjeev. *How to Cook Indian: More Than 500 Classic Recipes for the Modern Kitchen*. New York: Stewart, Tabori & Chang, 2011.

Larkcom, Joy. *Oriental Vegetables: The Complete Guide for the Gardening Cook*. 2nd ed. New York: Kodansha International, 2008.

Lee, Cecilia Hae-Jin. *Eating Korean*. Hoboken, NJ: John Wiley & Sons, 2005.

Lo, Kenneth. *New Chinese Cooking School*. New York: Crescent Books, 1995.

Mackey, Leslie, and Sallie Morris. *Illustrated Cook's Book of Ingredients: 2,500 of the World's Best with Classic Recipes*. 1st. U.S. ed. New York: DK Publishing, 2010.

Mouritsen, Ole G. *Seaweeds: Edible, Available & Sustainable*. Chicago: University of Chicago Press, 2013.

Nayak, Hari. *My Indian Kitchen: Preparing Delicious Indian Meals without Fear or Fuss*. North Clarendon, VT: Tuttle Publishing, 2011.

Nguyen, Andrea Quynhgiao. *Asian Dumpling: Mastering Gyoza, Spring Rolls, Samosas, and More*. Berkeley, CA: Ten Speed Press, 2009

Norman, Jill. *Herbs & Spices: The Cook's Reference*. New York: DK Publishing, 2002.

Oseland, James. *Cradle of Flavor: Home Cooking from the Spice Islands of Indonesia, Malaysia, and Singapore*. New York: W. W. Norton, 2006.

Owen, Sri. *Indonesian Regional Cooking*. New York: St. Martin's Press, 1994.

Punyaratabandhu, Leela. *Simple Thai Food: Classic Recipes from the Thai Home Kitchen*. Berkeley, CA: Ten Speed Press, 2014

Purewal, Jasjit. *Authentic Recipes from India*. Singapore: Periplus, 2004.

Riely, Elizabeth. *The Chef's Companion: A Culinary Dictionary*. 3rd ed. Hoboken, NJ: John Wiley & Sons, 2003.

Rinzler, Carol Ann. *The New Complete Book of Herbs, Spices, and Condiments*. New York: Checkmark Books, 2001.

Rolland, Jacques L, and Carol Sherman. *The Food Encyclopedia*. Toronto: Robert Rose, 2006.

Schneider, Elizabeth. *Uncommon Fruits & Vegetables: A Commonsense Guide*. New York: William Morrow, 1998.

Schmitz, Puangkram C., and Michael J. Worman. *Practical Thai Cooking*. New York: Kodansha International, 1985.

Selva Rajah, Carol. *Heavenly Fragrance: Cooking with Aromatic Asian Herbs, Fruits, Spices, and Seasonings*. Singapore: Periplus, 2007.

Shurtleff, William, and Akiko Aoyagi. *The Book of Miso*. 2nd ed. Berkeley, Ten Speed Press, 2001.

Simmons, Marie. *The Amazing World of Rice*. New York: HarperCollins, 2003.

Sinclair, Charles G. *International Dictionary of Food & Cooking*. Chicago: Fitzroy Dearborn Publishers, 1998.

Skelly, Carole J. *Dictionary of Herbs, Spice, Seasonings, and Natural Flavorings*. New York: Garland Publishing, 1994.

Solomon, Charmaine. *Charmaine Solomon's The Complete Asian Cookbook*. Rutland, VT: Tuttle Publishing, 2005.

Solomon, Charmaine. *Encyclopedia of Asian Food*. With Nina Solomon. Sydney, Australia: New Holland Publishers, 2010.

Song, Young Jin. *The Korean Kitchen*. London: Southwater, 2010.

Stobart, Tom. *The Cook's Encyclopedia: Ingredients and Processes*. New York: Harper & Row, 1981.

Takahashi, Yoko I. *The Tokyo Diet*. With Bruce Cassiday. New York: William Morrow, 1985.

Teubner, Christian, Eckart Witzigmann, and Tony Khoo. *The Rice Bible*. North Vancouver, BC: Viking Studio, 1999.

The Illustrated Cook's Book of Ingredients: 2,500 of the World's Best with Classic Recipes. 1st. U.S. ed. New York: DK Publishing, 2010.

Thompson, David. *Classic Thai Cuisine*. Berkeley, CA: Ten Speed Press, 1993.

Triêu, Thi Choi, and Marcel Isaak. *The Food of Vietnam: Authentic Recipes from the Heart of Indochina*. Singapore: Periplus, 1997.

Tsuji, Shizuo. *Japanese Cooking: A Simple Art*. 25th anniv. ed. With Mary Sutherland. New York: Kodansha International, 2006.

Wickramasinghe, Priya, and Carol Selva Rajah. *The Food of India*. London: Murdock Books, 2002.

Other Books by Jean B. MacLeod

If I'd Only Listened to My Mom, I'd Know How to Do This: Hundreds of Household Remedies

The Waste-Wise Kitchen Companion: Hundreds of Practical Tips for Repairing, Reusing, and Repurposing Food

The Waste-Wise Gardener: Tips and Techniques to Save Time, Money, and Energy While Creating the Garden of Your Dreams

The Kitchen Paraphernalia Handbook: Hundreds of Substitutions for Common (and Not-So-Common) Utensils, Gadgets, Tools, and Techniques

Seasoning Substitutions
Swaps and Stand-ins for Sweet or Savory Condiments and Flavorings

Baking Substitutions
The A-Z of Common, Unique, and Hard-to-Find Ingredients

Printed in Great Britain
by Amazon